New England SHIPBUILDING

VESSELS THAT MADE HISTORY

GLENN A. KNOBLOCK

THE
History
PRESS

Published by The History Press
Charleston, SC
www.historypress.com

First published 2021

Manufactured in the United States

ISBN 9781467147088

Library of Congress Control Number: 2021931150

*For my father, William Knoblock,
A member of the Housatonic Boat Club in Stratford, Connecticut, as a young
man and sailor on Long Island Sound long before I was born.*

William "Bill" Knoblock (*left*) and cousin Bud Van Giesen sailing in the
early 1950s. *Knoblock–Van Giesen family photo.*

CONTENTS

NOTES

Since this book is intended as a broad overview of shipbuilding in New England, versus a scholarly work, some of the below notes may be helpful. In regard to nautical terminology, the term *ship* as used here is a broadly defined one meaning any vessel designed to travel on or under the ocean or any body of water, propelled by sail or engine power and made of wood, iron or steel, or any combination thereof. For sailing vessels, there are many terms used to describe them, based on their sailing plans, while other vessels, particularly warships, are defined not for their sail plan but for the armament they carry or type of operations they conduct. Throughout the text, I have sought to define each vessel, so the reader need not be an expert as to all the ship types that exist.

The technical size of a ship is also very confusing to many a reader. The terms *ton* or *tonnage* are the most common in use throughout the book. Their exact meaning has evolved over time as ships themselves have changed, but they generally have two meanings. In regard to a cargo-carrying vessel, its registered tonnage is a reflection of its available interior space and resulting cargo carrying capacity. However, for non-cargo-carrying vessels like ships of war, their standard tonnage is a reflection of their size, and therefore weight, based on the amount of their water displacement.

In regard to U.S. naval vessels, the prefix of USS ("United States Ship") before a given vessel's commissioned name was not formalized until 1907. Therefore, during the American Revolution and subsequent naval wars, such ships as the *Ranger* or the *Constitution* were not referred to in this manner but rather by their ship type, i.e. the frigate *Constitution* or the sloop-of-war *Ranger*. The reader will also note that twentieth-century naval vessels have a letter and numerical designation in parenthesis after their name, such as USS *Massachusetts* (BB-59). The letters refer to the class of ship—BB for battleships, DD for destroyers, SS for submarines, CA for heavy cruisers, CL for light cruisers, CV for aircraft carriers and so on—while the numerals refer to the vessel's hull number, which was assigned upon building and is important both in identifying an individual ship when two or more vessels have carried the same name in the navy and in identifying its sequence of building in a class of ships.

Finally, no one book can cover the history of shipbuilding in New England in a comprehensive manner, but there have been published over the years numerous authoritative works that cover the subject in a given state or region or by vessel type or era. At the back of this book will be found a source bibliography that lists the works I have quoted and consulted while writing this book.

INTRODUCTION

*T*he America of today is a vast and powerful country with the largest and most important economy in the world. However, it hasn't always been thus; in the beginning, with the establishment of the first colonial settlements beginning in 1607, we were tied to the sea. Clinging to a foothold on the Atlantic coastline, our early settlers relied on ships for their very lives. Not only did these ships bring valuable supplies and settlers from England to help sustain the colonies' very existence, but also, within a decade, they were used to transport goods from one colony to another, all the way from the coast of Maine to English outposts in the Caribbean and back to the home country. Indeed, early America was a seafaring nation in every sense of the word, and it was shipbuilding that brought us our early wealth. New England was not only where the first ship was constructed by Englishmen in the New World, but the region has also remained a leader in shipbuilding over four hundred years later.

This book provides a broad overview of that shipbuilding history, presented through my choice of what I have deemed the seventy most notable ships built here and a telling of their story and achievements. As to the criteria used to choose these vessels, a variety of factors were considered, including being the first built or last survivor of a particular type of ship; unusual construction details; notable performance in terms of speed, endurance, service or other like factors; those involved in major maritime disasters; and, of course, close association with notable historic events, whether in peacetime or during war. Some vessels may have met only one of these criteria, while others checked off more than one box. My choice of which ships to highlight will be, no doubt, a source of dispute to some readers, and it may be that one ship could easily be substituted for another in some cases. Whether you're a maritime history enthusiast, someone who has a passing interest in the subject or perhaps are new to the subject, there are some interesting stories and little-known facts that await your discovery—an armchair nautical voyage, if you will! Finally, it should also be noted that historic ships aren't just found in the dusty pages of old books or in specialized maritime museums. No, they are also a part of our national conscience and even part of our popular culture. This is well evident in the hit folk song "The Wreck of the *Edmund Fitzgerald*" by Canadian singer Gordon Lightfoot. However, I prefer the title of a classic album by the rock-and-roll artist Tom Petty, *Damn the Torpedoes*, which borrows a line that originated from the deck of a Civil War warship, discussed in this volume. To complete that legendary battle cry, it's time now to get into our subject, "full speed ahead!"

Chapter 1

COLONIAL-ERA SHIPS, 1607–1775

The beginning of the shipbuilding industry started slowly and first came about out of reasons of both necessity and trade. The first ship ever built in America by European settlers came about in 1607, when the soon-to-fail Popham Colony, located at the mouth of the Kennebec River in what is now the town of Phippsburg, Maine, built its own vessel. This colony, also known as the Sagadahoc Colony, was formed by the Virginia Company of Plymouth, and the territory it was granted overlapped with that of the Virginia Company of London, which founded the rival colony of Jamestown, established to the south just months before as the first successful colony in America. The Popham Colony was led by Captain George Popham, who commanded the ship *Gift of God*, which brought the colonists to the Maine coast in August 1607. Like many of the early American settlements, the Popham Colony did not land until late in the summer, giving the settlers little time to prepare for the harsh New England weather. Though they did succeed in building a large fort, their dealings with the Abenaki Indians in the area did not go well, and no cooperation was established. Early in the winter, in December 1607, half of the colonists returned home to England, while those who stayed suffered through a terrible winter. Their leader, Captain Popham, died in February 1608, leaving a young Raleigh Gilbert, nephew to Sir Walter Raleigh, in charge. The rest of the colonists abandoned the site in August 1608, with the colony lasting just a year.

VIRGINIA

The only notable achievement of the Popham Colony was the building of the *Virginia*, a small pinnace about sixty feet long and of about thirty tons, the first ship ever built in America. It took three months to build, demonstrating that a colony, with the right men, could make a success of shipbuilding in America using readily available timber. The only contemporary image of the *Virginia* is that drawn by a surveyor in the colony who made a plan of the fort that was built and included a representation of a ship presumed to be the one that they built. Though small, the *Virginia* was a sturdy vessel. Not only did she transport the remaining colonists, forty-five in number, back to England, but she also made two subsequent round-trip voyages to America from England, helping supply the Jamestown Colony in 1609 and 1610. After this time, the ship disappears from the records, but with her place in American shipbuilding history firmly established.

No other ship was built in America until the establishment of the Plymouth Colony, in what would become Massachusetts, in 1620. The Pilgrims in Plymouth, first brought here by the *Mayflower*, had a very rough time in establishing a foothold. However, while substantial shipbuilding activities would take a decade to establish, this does not mean that no watercraft were fashioned during these intervening years. Of those small boats that were built, most were of a small type called a shallop, which measured about fifteen to twenty feet long and was propelled by oars and had a mast with a single sail. Because of their shallow draft, only about two feet, they were only suitable for traveling close to shore, and early colonists still relied on ships from England to bring them supplies or trade farther afield. Within a short time, subsequent settlers at places like Dover, New Hampshire (1623), established by fishing merchants, and at Salem, Massachusetts (1626), began to build more durable, albeit still small vessels.

This 1957-issued U.S. postage stamp features an artist's rendition of the pinnace *Virginia*, the first ship built by European settlers in the New World. *Author's collection.*

BLESSING OF THE BAY

The establishment of the Massachusetts Bay Colony took place at Boston in 1630, with its initial seven hundred colonists arriving aboard the Winthrop Fleet of eleven ships, followed by six other ships later that year. These arrivals provided not only the financial means but also the skilled labor to begin the shipbuilding industry on a larger scale. Within a year, in July 1631, the third known ship to be built in America, the *Blessing of the Bay*, was launched in the Mystic River for Governor John Winthrop, built by Robert Moulton and a company of shipbuilders sent by the colony from England in 1629. It is interesting that the vessel was launched on July 4, designed as a trader but also armed so that it could defend itself from pirates. Indeed, the year after she was built, colonists in Portsmouth called for the use of the ship in fighting off the pirate Dixie Bull. The *Blessing of the Bay* was an important ship, it being built by the head of the Massachusetts Bay Colony with the intent of both trading with the Dutch and expediting communication with the colony at New Amsterdam (New York), as the sea route was much easier than traveling on foot through the wilderness between the two colonies. It was also hoped that the ship would trade with the coastal colony at Jamestown and even farther afield. The ship sailed on her maiden voyage under the command of Captain Anthony Dike to New Amsterdam in August 1631, serving as a voyager thereafter for the next five years or so, likely making a great profit for her owner. Her common cargo included salt, lumber products and even maple sugar. In exchange, the Dutch provided spices from the Far East as well as sugar and molasses from the West Indies, a trade that New England would soon come to dominate because of the many ships it built.

DESIRE

Following the building of the *Blessing of the Bay*, the growth of the shipbuilding industry in New England proceeded rapidly. All along the coast at Portsmouth, New Hampshire; and Gloucester, Marblehead, Salem, Boston, and Scituate, Massachusetts, ships between 30 and 50 tons were beginning to be built quite regularly, while ships over 100 tons in size were no longer unusual. One from Marblehead, the *Desire*, was a 120-ton vessel built in 1636. She would cement that town's early reputation as a shipbuilding center but also would soon occupy a darker place in New England history. The ship was built for fishing on the Grand Banks but also took part in the West Indies trade. However, two years later, in 1638, the *Desire*, commanded by Captain William Pierce, returned from a months-long voyage to the West Indies with a cargo of tobacco, cotton and human beings. They were African slaves from the Providence Island colony, established by English Puritans in 1629 and lasting until it was captured by the Spanish in 1641. Though records are uncertain, the *Desire* was among the first, if not the first, slave ships to operate from New England. Sadly, many more would follow in her wake until the slave trade was made illegal in 1807.

Through the rest of the colonial era, well-built and increasingly larger ships would be built in New England. By 1641, "a veritable monster" of three hundred tons was built at Salem, cementing that town's reputation as a seaport for the next two hundred years. Little is known of the shipbuilding activities in Rhode Island. As for Connecticut, the Dutch colonized what is now Hartford in 1633, but there seems to have been no sizeable vessels built by them. The English planted colonies in Windsor and Wethersfield in 1634 and at New Haven in 1638. It was on the mighty Connecticut River, not along coastal Connecticut, that the shipbuilding industry got its start in the state. The first ship said to be built in Connecticut was the *Tryall*, built at Wethersfield in 1649 by Thomas Deming, a shipwright who came from Boston and established his yard on Wethersfield Cove, an oxbow in the Connecticut River. Indeed, New England accomplished in less than fifty years, beginning with the *Virginia* in 1607, what it took the English hundreds of years to achieve in terms of vessel size. Shipbuilders in colonial America were growing the trade and the size of their ships at such a rapid pace that even the British Royal Navy, as well as merchants overseas in England and Scotland, soon began to order vessels from shipwrights in New England.

HMS *Falkland*

The first entity to actually contract for a ship to be built in America was the Royal Navy when, in 1690, it ordered the building of the HMS *Falkland* at Portsmouth, New Hampshire. The ship, which was launched in 1696, was built by Thomas Holland and was a fifty-gun fourth-rate ship. Upon completion, she was not only the first true naval vessel built in America but also the first Royal Navy ship to be built here. The ship was a sizeable one, measuring in at 638 tons and was 129 feet long. This ship would put

Portsmouth on the map as a center of naval construction, a tradition that is carried on even today. Portsmouth was a natural choice for shipbuilding not just due to its fine harbor and deep river site but also because the forests of New Hampshire, like those in Maine, were renowned for their seemingly endless stands of white pine and white oak. The HMS *Falkland* would go on to have an eminently successful and long naval career. She was employed not only in escorting merchant ships to and from America, but in 1704, in company with another ship-of-the-line engaged the thirty-six-gun French ship *La Seine* off the Azores. After her capture, she was renamed HMS *Falkland Prize*. She was taken out of active service in 1768. Interestingly, the HMS *Falkland* was not the last Royal Navy ship built at Portsmouth before 1700; in 1698, the thirty-four-gun fifth-rate ship HMS *Bedford Galley* was also built by Holland, her career lasting until 1725, while in 1749, the HMS *America* was built by Colonel Nathaniel Meserve, she being a fifty-gun fifth-rate ship-of-the-line.

MINERVA

This ship highlights the mast trade that developed in northern New England during the colonial era, continuing to the outbreak of the American Revolution. The one-thousand-ton mast ship *Minerva* was built by British merchants at Falmouth, Maine (now Portland), in 1775. She was perhaps the epitome of that type of ship, designed to carry a load of 120-foot-long sticks of white pine timber, designated for use as masts for the ships of the Royal Navy. These mast trees were loaded through ports that were cut in the stern, the open hold being specially designed for the purpose. The ship-timber trade for Royal Navy use got its start early on in America, when a mast ship carried a load from Virginia in 1609. The two major centers for the mast trade in colonial America were on the Piscataqua River at Portsmouth, New Hampshire, and at Falmouth, Maine, on Casco Bay. The forests in these areas contained white pine trees that grew straight and tall up to 200 feet in height, with diameters at ground level of as much as forty-two inches— perfect for the masts of Royal Navy vessels. In particular, New Hampshire pine trees were a coveted commodity, and the forests of New England as a whole were considered by the British the best in the world for mast trees, as well as for the shorter pine and oak trees that provided other wooden shipbuilding components. This importance was made official in 1691, when a law was passed reserving all such trees on land not previously granted that measured twenty-four inches or greater in circumference at the base as the property of the British Crown, with surveyors to be sent out to mark the bark of such trees with the King's Broad Arrow to let all know that such timber was untouchable. For those unauthorized to cut such trees, a large fine was to be paid. In New Hampshire, the law became even more onerous when, in 1722, the royal government passed a law reserving trees with a diameter of twelve inches or more for Crown use. These laws, of course, did not sit well with the colonists in New Hampshire or Maine, and in some locales, armed confrontations between settlers and the king's surveyors, called mast tree riots, broke out, including at Exeter (now Fremont) in 1734 and at Goffstown and Weare in 1772.

The *Minerva* was a British-owned ship, commanded by Captain Thomas Coulson, and her building was finished under the watchful eye of the Royal Navy. They provided the escort for the ship that brought the *Minerva*'s rigging and other supplies from England. However, when she was complete, serious problems began because she could not get a cargo, as local Patriots were hiding the annual supply of masts in a small cove away from British authorities in May 1775. The *Minerva* had previously hoped to get a cargo from Portsmouth but was prevented from doing so by Patriots there. Patriots in Maine would eventually be punished by the Royal Navy in October 1775 when a British fleet bombarded and burned Falmouth, destroying hundreds of homes and buildings. As for the *Minerva*, I have not been able to determine her fate; the Maine Patriots may have succeeded in destroying the mast ship, or she may have sailed to Boston under the protection of the Royal Navy. As for her intended mast cargo, they remained in the cove in which they had been hidden, never to see a Royal dockyard, and there slowly rotted away for many years. It has often been stated that even for one hundred years after the American Revolution, trees in New Hampshire and Maine forests could still be seen marked with the King's Broad Arrow. The only remnant of the mast trade today are the many byways named "Mast Road" or "Mast Landing Road" in the area, marking the routes and places where these mast trees were dragged through the wilderness by teams of oxen or the places they were landed and gathered prior to shipment.

Chapter 2

NAVAL AND PRIVATEER SHIPS OF THE AMERICAN REVOLUTION, 1775–1780

*T*he naval aspect of the American Revolution is a subject that is little understood by most Americans, while most of the ships themselves are virtually unknown. This is certainly understandable as, unlike the War of 1812, few important or dramatic sea actions were fought, and only one man, Captain John Paul Jones, gained achievements that have resonated with the general public in the intervening two-plus centuries. However, this does not mean that the war at sea was inconsequential. Several factors regarding the naval war must be considered from the outset, the first being that the war at sea was actually fought at two levels: one on a privately funded basis and one that was funded by the Continental Congress. That part of the war on the seas that was privately funded was fought by a group of ships called privateers. Vessels in this class were privately owned and operated with no military orders to guide their operations. Instead, these ships were given a letter of marque by either their state colonial government or the Continental Congress, a formal commission that authorized the vessel in question to cruise against the enemy at will and capture prizes. The proceeds from the sale of these captured vessels and their cargos was split among the ship owner and his crew. This letter of marque made such cruises legal in terms of the laws of the sea then in effect, for without it, such a vessel would be called a pirate ship, and, if captured, its crew could be put to death. As historian Edgar Maclay recounts, privateers ranged greatly in size, from the one-gun schooner *Two Brothers* of Salem (25-man crew) to the twenty-two-gun *Hampden* of New Hampshire (150-man crew), and their role was not to attack ships of the Royal Navy but rather British merchant ships that were carrying supplies to America. By capturing these merchant ships, they thus wrought havoc on the British supply line and made the enemy's efforts in fighting the war much more difficult and, ultimately, unsuccessful. As with naval ships, many privateers were captured by the British, some were lost at sea, but many also achieved outstanding results. As for the ships of the Continental navy, they had an uphill battle from the start; the British Royal Navy was the most powerful naval force in the world, being well manned with experienced commanders. In contrast, in the beginning there was no American navy, period. The procurement of fighting ships, the establishment of a command and supply structure and the raising of funds to accomplish these goals all had to be done quickly and on the fly. The results of these efforts were a mixed bag at best.

HANNAH

The first naval ships were not ordered by the Continental navy, which was not formally established until October 13, 1775, but acquired by General George Washington. All of the ships in Washington's navy were merchant ships, purchased and commissioned as warships. The first of the ships acquired by Washington and commissioned to cruise against the British was the *Hannah*, a schooner owned by Marblehead merchant and Continental army regimental commander Colonel John Glover. Other than the fact that the *Hannah* was employed as a fishing schooner and was named after Glover's daughter, nothing is known of the vessel in terms of size and when or where she was built, despite much speculation. However, her true importance lies in the fact that she is considered by many to be the founding vessel of the U.S. Navy. Even before its formal establishment, Washington commissioned Captain Nicholas Broughton, an officer in Glover's regiment, to take command of the *Hannah* at Beverly on September 2 and cruise against the enemy in hopes of damaging the British supply line. Three days later, Broughton departed port but soon was pursued by two enemy ships, including the twenty-gun HMS *Lively*, and retreated to Gloucester. Heading back to sea very quickly, the *Hannah* encountered and captured the HMS *Unity*. This vessel was the first prize ever captured by an American naval vessel. The *Unity* was subsequently brought into Gloucester, and the *Hannah* would depart on another cruise, only to be run aground at Beverly

Formerly a merchant ship owned by John Glover of Marblehead, the *Hannah* was the first commissioned naval vessel of the United States in 1775. *Courtesy Naval History and Heritage Command archives.*

after a four-hour running battle with the sixteen-gun sloop HMS *Nautilus* on October 10, 1775. After this action, the fate of the *Hannah* is a mystery. Though she was not heavily damaged as a result of going aground, she never served as a naval vessel again, perhaps returning to her merchant career after the war's end.

While the Continental navy at first used converted merchant ships to perform sea duty, in December 1775, the Continental Congress ordered the building of thirteen frigates, five of them armed with thirty-two guns, five with twenty-eight and three with twenty-four. They were to be ready to put to sea in March 1776. Of these thirteen ships, two were assigned to be built in Massachusetts, two in Rhode Island, two in Connecticut and one in New Hampshire. The designer of the original seven frigates to be built in New England was Joshua Humphreys of Pennsylvania, but, as naval historian Howard I. Chapelle has documented, almost none were built exactly to his plans because of a delay in getting the plans sent out to the various states. The fact that these ships were built at all during a time of war makes them worthy of remembrance as a group, even if most of them were either captured or lost during their short service and Continental navy leadership was often severely lacking.

PROVIDENCE

The first of the Continental frigates to be completed was probably the twenty-eight-gun *Providence*, built by Sylvester Bowers of Providence, Rhode Island. Launched in May 1776, she would have a long delay in outfitting and was blockaded in the Providence River by the British. She was commanded by Captain Abraham Whipple, known for his daring destruction of the customs schooner HMS *Gaspee* off Warwick, Rhode Island, in 1772. On the night of April 30, 1778, Whipple guided *Providence* past the British blockade under heavy fire and headed out to sea, heading directly to France to bring back supplies and guns for the other frigates under construction. Sailing back in company with the frigate *Boston*, the two ships captured three ships during the return voyage, subsequently arriving at Portsmouth, New Hampshire, in October. *Providence* then went to Boston to get a new crew, sailing from there in June 1779 as flagship of a small fleet that also included the *Ranger*. The fleet operated in Caribbean waters before arriving off Charleston, South Carolina, in defense of that city. When Charleston fell to the British in May 1780, a number of American naval ships were captured there, including the *Providence*. Commanded by an able officer, the *Providence*, despite her capture, was a relatively successful vessel.

HANCOCK

At Newburyport, Massachusetts, two of the authorized frigates were built: the thirty-two-gun *Hancock* and the twenty-four-gun *Boston*. Both were built by Jonathan Greenleaf and Stephen and Ralph Cross and launched in June 1776. The *Hancock* was commanded by Captain John Manley and was probably the finest and fastest of the thirteen frigates that were built, while the smaller *Boston* was commanded by Captain Hector McNeill. Sailing together, both ships departed Boston after gathering a crew and supplies in late May 1777. Their cruise was an initial success, as they captured the twenty-eight-gun frigate HMS *Fox* in June after a running battle. However, the success of the American frigates was short-lived, for on July 7, the two, with their prize in tow, encountered the forty-four-gun HMS *Rainbow*, thirty-gun HMS *Flora* and ten-gun brig HMS *Victor* off Cape Sable, Nova Scotia. The HMS *Fox*, now manned by Americans, was cut loose and recaptured by the British after a fierce battle, while *Hancock* tried to outrun the British

The frigates *Boston* and *Hancock* battling Royal Navy warships. The *Boston*, partially obscured by cannon smoke, is at center left. *Courtesy Naval History and Heritage Command archives.*

squadron, only to be overhauled after a thirty-nine-hour chase. With the broadsides of the British ships doing damage, Captain Manley was forced to strike his colors and surrender his ship. The *Hancock* was subsequently taken into the Royal Navy and renamed HMS *Iris*, immediately recognized as the fastest frigate in the fleet. She would have a successful career, capturing an American frigate before being captured by the French off the Virginia coast in 1781 while supporting Lord Cornwallis at Yorktown.

RANGER

A more successful warship built at Portsmouth was the eighteen-gun sloop of war *Ranger*. Launched in May 1777 at Langdon's shipyard and built by James Hackett, her commander was the famed Scotsman Captain John Paul Jones. While Jones oversaw her building and outfitting, he was not in love with the *Ranger*. Indeed, unlike the frigates, she was said to be a slow and cranky ship, hard to handle. Unlike many other commanders, Jones was anxious to get to sea, and there would be no dawdling. She first sailed for France in November 1777, carrying dispatches to the American commissioners in Paris and, along the way, capturing two prizes. While in Nantes, Jones and the *Ranger*, which flew the new Stars and Stripes American

This 1892 painting by Edward Moran features the eighteen-gun sloop of war *Ranger*, built at Portsmouth, New Hampshire. *Courtesy Naval History and Heritage Command archives.*

flag, received an official salute from the French fleet, the first time the new flag was so honored. In May 1778, Jones departed Brest for the Irish Sea, bringing the fight to British home waters. The *Ranger* captured several prizes and landed marines ashore to raid the British port of Whitehaven. For the first time, the British people were experiencing the war firsthand, with Jones's depredations creating a panic. Off Carrickfergus, Ireland, the *Ranger* fought and captured the fourteen-gun HMS *Drake* and captured yet another prize before returning to France in early May. From there, Jones was promoted to the command of the *Bonhomme Richard* and would soon have his epic and historic fight with HMS *Serapis*. (We shall hear more of his exploits in a short while.) Meanwhile, the command of the *Ranger* fell to Jones's first officer, Lieutenant Thomas Simpson. He departed France for Portsmouth in August 1778 in company of the frigates *Providence* and *Boston*, and the squadron captured three prizes along the way. The *Ranger* subsequently made two cruises in the North Atlantic in 1779 in company with the *Queen of France* and *Providence* and *Warren*, they capturing fifteen prizes worth over $1 million. The *Ranger* was sent south to Charleston in December 1779 and helped to capture several prizes but was ultimately captured herself when the city fell to British forces in May 1780.

TRUMBULL

Today, the landscape has changed so much and so many bridges cross the Connecticut River, it's hard to believe that any sizeable vessels could be launched on its waters, but they were. One of these was the thirty-gun frigate *Trumbull*, built by John Cotton at Chatham (now Portland). The ship was launched in September 1776 and made its way down to the mouth of the river at Old Saybrook, but here she was in trouble. Because the seven-hundred-ton ship had a deep draft, she could not get across the sandbar that had developed at the entrance to Long Island Sound, so she required assistance to get to sea. Here the *Trumbull* was stuck for three years. Finally, in 1779, the ship was able to clear the sandbar by unusual means and thence proceeded to New London for her final fitting-out. Under command of Captain James Nicholson, the frigate finally began her first cruise in late May 1780 and soon saw her first action when, on June 1, she spotted the thirty-two-gun British privateer *Watt*. After mistaking the American ship for a British frigate, the *Watt* soon came in close contact, with the resulting confrontation becoming the hardest-fought naval battle of the entire war. Nearly equally armed, the ships battled each other for over two hours at close range—less than one hundred yards—and at one time were locked together while exchanging gunfire. When the smoke cleared, the *Watt* was badly shot up and in a sinking condition, suffering thirteen killed and seventy-nine wounded, while the *Trumbull* suffered eight killed, including two marine lieutenants, and thirteen wounded, with two of her three masts shot away. Nicholson wanted to pursue the *Watt* as she limped away, but the condition of his ship and crew would not allow this, so the battle was ultimately a draw. The *Trumbull*, after making repairs at sea, sailed to Philadelphia, where Nicholson was recognized for his gallantry. The *Trumbull* was stuck at Philadelphia due to a lack of supplies and would not head out to sea again until August 1781. Departing in company with two heavily armed privateers and tasked with protecting a large convoy of supply ships, the group late in the month encountered two vessels, the HMS *Iris* (the former American frigate *Hancock*) and a heavily armed British privateer. A chase ensued, but during a sudden nighttime rain squall, the *Trumbull* had some of her top-masts damaged, and soon the British ships caught up with her. Too damaged to escape, Captain Nicholson prepared his frigate for a fight and engaged the *Iris* for over an hour. However, with casualties mounting and a second British ship ready to enter the fight, Nicholson decided to strike his flag, and the *Trumbull* surrendered. She was

This 1780-dated gravestone in the Granary Burial Ground in Boston features an image of the frigate *Trumbull*, on which the deceased was wounded. *Author's collection.*

then towed into New York, barely able to make port, and here disappears from history. The *Trumbull* holds the distinction of being the last of the original thirteen frigates authorized by the Continental Congress to be lost during the war.

ALLIANCE

The thirty-six-gun *Alliance* was built under a later congressional authorization and was launched at Amesbury, Massachusetts, in April 1778. She was built by William and James Hackett, who also helped build the *Raleigh* and *Ranger* at Portsmouth, and was originally intended to be named *Hancock*, after the frigate lost in 1777, but had her name changed to *Alliance* in honor of the French, who had entered the war as an American ally. Her command was given to Captain Pierre Landais, a man who hoped to become to the American navy what the Marquis de Lafayette had become to the army—a valuable ally and brave and competent officer who became a friend to George Washington. This frigate, however, had a maddening career, and though she would turn out to be the only vessel to survive the war intact and in Continental navy service, Landais was an unhinged character who did more harm than good with what was reputed to be one of the finest frigates afloat at the time of her building. Trouble began almost at the very start of Landais's command, but the situation worsened and finally came to a head during the Battle of Flamborough Head, off the British coast, on September 23, 1779. Captain John Paul Jones in *Bonhomme Richard* and his squadron, including *Alliance*, engaged the forty-four-gun HMS *Serapis* and the twenty-two-gun *Countess of Scarborough*. Landais took little part in the action and instead left Jones to battle the British. Landais only fired the *Alliance*'s guns once the *Serapis* and *Bonhomme Richard* were grappled together and engaged in close-fighting, during which Jones, when asked to surrender, proclaimed his now-immortal words: "I have not yet begun to fight."

The fire of the *Alliance* severely damaged both ships and left the *Bonhomme Richard* in a sinking condition. As a result, Jones transferred his command to *Serapis* after her captain had surrendered, and after repairs were made at sea, the squadron, *Alliance* included, headed for Holland, making Texel

The thirty-six-gun frigate *Alliance*, built at Amesbury, Massachusetts, in 1778. *Courtesy Naval History and Heritage Command archives.*

in early October. Here, Jones relieved Landais of command of the *Alliance*, but the Frenchman, prior to the voyage back to Boston, took command of the ship with the help of political supporters. On the voyage home, Landais finally lost it completely, alienating his crew and even those who previously supported him, and was relieved of command. Arriving in Boston in September, he was forcibly removed from *Alliance* and dismissed, finally, from the navy. Command of the *Alliance* fell to Captain John Barry, and after being put in fighting trim, she made several cruises in the North Atlantic in early 1781, capturing a number of prizes before returning to Boston. Later, the frigate was in Philadelphia when the war ended. She twice tried to depart that port for France but was in poor condition and both times returned to port, the last time in August 1783. Due to a lack of funds, *Alliance* was left to languish in Philadelphia before finally being sold to private parties in August 1785. With her sale, the Continental navy was finally disbanded, without any ships and no funds to build such for a peacetime navy. The *Alliance* subsequently made at least one voyage as a merchant ship but was abandoned sometime after 1788 at Petty Island in the Delaware River, where her timbers rotted away in the sand and were visible for over one hundred years.

OUR FINAL NOTABLE VESSEL in this chapter brings us back to the privateer ships of the American Revolution. These vessels sailed from just about every port in New England, from the shores of Connecticut all the way up to Maine, and it is estimated by historian Charles Lampson that close to seventy thousand men served in at least two thousand ships, armed with no fewer than twenty thousand guns. In contrast, the navy ultimately operated just fifty-three ships of all types, manned by fewer than four thousand men and carrying fewer than three thousand guns in aggregate. While the exploits of the privateers have become increasingly well documented, they still remain largely forgotten.

GRAND TURK

The three-hundred-ton *Grand Turk* is a good example of a New England–built privateer. She was owned by the highly successful merchant Elias Hasket Derby and others of Salem—a premier port known for its privateers—but was built on contract at the North River shipyard in Hanover of Thomas Barstow. Interestingly, the shrewd Derby paid for his privateer via barter with goods like rum and butter, which were often in short supply during the war. Built specifically as a privateer, the *Grand Turk* was the first Salem ship to bear this name but, as will be noted later, not the last. Her hull was sheathed in copper, so as to prevent marine growth and make her an even faster sailer, and she was first armed with twenty-eight cannons. Launched in May 1781, she sailed on her first cruise in late June after having quickly recruited a crew of 140 men. It should be noted that while a normal merchant vessel would not have such a large crew, the heavily armed privateers needed them for two reasons: to man their gun crews and, most importantly, to have the available manpower to crew captured ships so that they could be sent into a port intact to be disposed of at auction. After all, it was the ultimate goal of a privateer owner to sell the proceeds of his captures to not only cover the expenses of the operation but also to make a profit. Even a ship as fine as the *Grand Turk*, it was hoped, would not face a Royal Navy frigate, and no responsible privateer captain would attempt such an engagement, even if heavily armed, unless the circumstances absolutely required it. As a result, while privateers did have some rousing engagements at times, many of their cruises resulted in the peaceful capture of enemy supply ships, with the very presence of a twenty-eight-gun ship like the *Grand Turk* a deterrence against resistance.

On her first cruise, the Salem privateer captured in the course of three months' time three vessels, including a sixteen-gun brig, before returning to port. For her second cruise beginning in October 1781, the guns were reduced to twenty-four and her crew reduced to one hundred men, and almost immediately, she returned to port with a prize: the fourteen-gun brig *Providence*. The *Grand Turk* departed port again in late October on her third cruise, one that took place in European waters over fourteen months and netted eight valuable prizes. In all, through the end of the war in April 1783, the *Grand Turk* made eleven sorties, capturing twenty-five vessels worth hundreds of thousands of dollars. As historian Lampson has noted, the British overall during the war suffered losses valued at as much as $60 million, with 10 percent of their troop and supply ships lost on the high seas. It was mostly privateers like the *Grand Turk* that made this a painful reality. In peacetime, the *Grand Turk* would continue to serve her owners for many years as a successful merchant vessel. It is therefore not surprising that many landmarks around Salem have been named after this vessel over the years, including the Grand Turk Tavern, the Grand Turk Inn and a road near the waterfront named Grand Turk Way.

Chapter 3

NAVAL AND PRIVATEER SHIPS
OF THE WAR OF 1812

*I*n this chapter, we continue our look at the early naval history of America, focusing on some of the ships that were built as part of the first permanent United States Navy and saw service in the War of 1812, as well as the privateer vessels that also played a large part in finally ending any plans the British may have had in regard to their former colonies. With the selling off of the frigate *Alliance* in 1785, the United States would have no naval ships for its protection, either at home or on the seas. Not only was there no will to develop the navy, but most importantly, there was no money to do so in the wake of the long-lasting and costly fight for independence. This situation could not even begin to change until our federal government was finally established in 1789 with the ratification of the Constitution, but even after this time, funding was nonexistent. The immediate postwar years, however, were a time when America's merchant vessels were expanding operations around the globe, with new trade relations being established. It was only then that the need for an American Navy began to be apparent. This was especially true in the Mediterranean, where ever-increasingly, American ships were obstructed in their trading activities along the Barbary Coast of North Africa (comprising modern-day Algeria, Libya, Tunisia and Morocco) by both pirates and armed vessels of such rulers as the Bey of Algiers. The regencies in these countries were vassals of the Ottoman Empire, and their military power was fairly weak. Because of this, they dared not prey on the shipping of European powers like Britain and France, but after the American Revolution, things changed. American traders were no longer under British protection, and that country even encouraged the Barbary states in their attacks on American vessels. With no navy, America was even weaker than the Barbary states and had no means to fight back to protect our interests. Diplomacy might work for a time but was largely ineffective and resulted in America paying a ransom, or tribute money, in order to redeem American sailors from captivity. Even worse, things came to a head in 1797, when a peace was agreed upon in return for America building for Algiers several naval vessels that we were to deliver into their hands to seal the deal. Though it seems astonishing to us today, this happened right here in New England, where the thirty-two-gun frigate *Crescent* was built at Portsmouth, New Hampshire, in 1797 as a penalty for not upholding our treaty agreement with Algiers. This fine ship set sail for Algiers in January 1798, her deliverance into their hands one of the most galling and shameful events in the history of our young and weak nation. It was also a clarion call for the building of a new American navy.

The beginnings of the new navy came from direct public pressure in 1791 to these overseas problems, with the result that the new navy would be established with two approaches. The first of these was actual government support through legislation that would allocate the needed funding, while the second was the addition of new ships to the navy of vessels by the building of such ships through private/public initiatives. First in importance were those six ships, three forty-four-gun and three thirty-six-gun frigates, two of which would be built in New England, that were authorized by the Naval Act of 1794. Some $688,888 was allocated for their building, with these ships since formally recognized as our first naval vessels. According to Howard Chapelle, their design was a collaboration between naval architects Joshua Humphreys (who helped design the Continental navy frigates), Josiah Fox and William Doughty, and what they came up with was a true marvel, a fast and large frigate for their day.

CONSTITUTION

The forty-four-gun frigate *Constitution* is probably the most well-known ship in American history and is today the world's oldest commissioned warship afloat, still serving the navy and manned by active-duty personnel. The 1,576-ton frigate was built at the shipyard of Edmund Hartt in Boston's North End. Her first commander, Captain Samuel Nicholson, a

Revolutionary War naval veteran, supervised the efforts. The hull, whose timbers are twenty-one inches thick, was stoutly built, her timbers being pine and live oak, while her mainmast soars 220 feet high. Her keel was laid down in November 1794, but construction was slow due to a lack of funds altogether and was halted in March 1796 when a peace treaty was signed with Algiers. However, after much debate and prompting by President Washington, construction was resumed and the *Constitution* was finally launched after a failed first attempt in October 1797. She first put to sea in July 1798 for service in the Quasi-War with France. This undeclared war was fought solely on the high seas between French and American naval vessels and privateers from 1798 to 1800. The *Constitution* performed well and captured a number of prizes, but in 1801, with the war over, she was laid up at Boston. She was eventually recommissioned in May 1803 under Captain Edward Preble as flagship for a new squadron being sent to the Mediterranean for service in the First Barbary War. After having her hull re-sheathed in copper supplied by Paul Revere, she departed Boston in August. While off the Straits of Gibraltar, she was confronted by a British warship, and though the situation was tense, Captain Preble refused to back down, and eventually the incident ended peacefully. While off the Barbary Coast, *Constitution* took part in the Battles of Tripoli Harbor and, after several months of battle in which the Tripolitan fleet was ravaged, a peace treaty was signed aboard *Constitution*. The frigate remained in the Mediterranean for four years before finally being relieved of duty and sent back home, arriving in Boston in October 1807. When war was declared in June 1812, *Constitution*, under the command of Captain Isaac Hull, departed Boston alone in July in an attempt to join the squadron of John Rodgers in the USS *President*, but when a squadron of British ships was sighted, he was forced to run, eluding them finally after a fifty-seven-hour chase. He returned to Boston. Fearful of being blockaded in port, Hull departed Boston in August, heading for the Gulf of St. Lawrence and capturing and burning three British merchant ships along the way. From these crews, Hull learned that there was a British frigate some one hundred miles to the south, so he set a new course and began stalking his prey. That frigate turned out to be the thirty-eight-gun HMS *Guerriere*, and within three days, the *Constitution* found her and Hull quickly maneuvered his ship into close position and gained the advantage, the enemy ship's opening salvo doing no real harm. After a full broadside wrecked the *Guerriere*'s mizzenmast and rendered her less maneuverable, she collided with *Constitution*, the two ships subsequently locked together in battle.

While both crews tried to board the other, neither was successful due to heavy seas. It was during this battle that *Constitution* gained her nickname… many British cannonballs simply bounced off the frigate's stout hull and did no damage. A crew member cried, "Huzzah! Her sides are made of iron." Thus it was that "Old Ironsides" became *Constitution*'s nickname for the ages. During the battle, *Constitution* continued to pour broadsides into the *Guerriere*, and when the two ships finally separated, the enemy frigate's remaining masts toppled over, leaving her a wallowing wreck, with close to a third of her crew killed or wounded. HMS *Guerriere* surrendered to a largely intact *Constitution* and, too badly damaged to tow into Boston as a prize, was subsequently burned. The American frigate arrived back in Boston in late August 1812, only to find that news of the battle had preceded them. Hull and his crew were hailed as heroes. Had she done nothing else, this capture alone cemented *Constitution*'s place in American naval history and lore.

Captain William Bainbridge next assumed command of *Constitution* and departed Boston in October 1812, heading for the British shipping lanes off the coast of Brazil. On December 29, she encountered the forty-six-gun HMS *Java*, that frigate's opening shot severely damaging the *Constitution*'s rigging. The two ships subsequently exchanged broadsides, with *Constitution*'s helm shot away, forcing the crew to rig a tiller so that she could be steered manually. The two frigates subsequently fell in close together, with Bainbridge wounded several times, while the *Constitution*'s broadsides brought down the *Java*'s foremast. Bainbridge subsequently withdrew from *Java* in order to effect repairs and, upon approaching *Java* an hour later, found her a floating wreck in no condition to fight. The *Java* surrendered without any further resistance and was subsequently burned because she was too damaged to bring into port, though her helm was salvaged and used on *Constitution*. The American frigate subsequently returned to Boston in February 1813, her commander and crew even greater heroes than before. This battle was important as it resulted in the third British frigate defeat in the months since the war began, two by *Constitution* and one by the frigate *United States*, which captured by HMS *Macedonian* in October. As a result, the British Admiralty ordered that frigate-versus-frigate action was to be avoided due to the heavy nature of the American frigates and that only more heavily armed ships-of-the-line were authorized to partake in such duels. However, the *Constitution* was not yet done fighting. She lay at Boston for nearly nine months, undergoing a refit, which took extra time due to a shortage of supplies.

The USS *Constitution* in Boston. July 4, 2014, firing a seventeen-gun salute. *Photo by Seaman Matthew R. Fairchild. Courtesy of the U.S. Navy.*

In December 1813, *Constitution* departed Boston, now commanded by Captain Charles Stewart, and headed for the West Indies to raid British shipping there. By March 1814, she had captured five merchant ships, as well as a fourteen-gun British warship, but when her mainmast was damaged off Bermuda, she headed back to the United States, pursued for a time by two British frigates before safely making the harbor at Marblehead, Massachusetts, and subsequently arriving in Boston. Here she lay blockaded in port until the end of the year, when Stewart was finally able to escape the harbor and head out to sea, eventually hunted by a British squadron that included the fifty-gun HMS *Leander*. Stewart and *Constitution* were off the coast of Spain in February 1815 when it was learned that the Treaty of Ghent had been signed, nominally ending the war, but not yet ratified. Later that month, he sighted two warships, the twenty-two-gun HMS *Cyane* and twenty-gun HMS *Levant*, and gave chase. Coming in close, *Constitution* engaged both ships, and when *Levant* was forced to withdraw for repairs, *Constitution* poured broadsides into *Cyane* until she surrendered. Captain Stewart subsequently gave chase to *Levant*, and after he pulled within range and gave her several broadsides, she, too, surrendered. *Constitution* and her prizes were headed to the Cape Verde Islands for port when the British squadron in pursuit finally caught up with *Constitution*. *Levant* was subsequently recaptured by the British, while *Cyane* and her prize crew made their getaway and subsequently made the United States, where *Cyane* served for many years as a U.S. Navy warship. As for *Constitution*, she once again eluded her pursuers and was heading for Brazil when it was learned that the peace treaty had been formally ratified.

Following the War of 1812, the *Constitution* served in the Mediterranean and the Pacific and was one of the most revered ships in the American fleet. When heavy repairs were required and it was rumored that she was to be scrapped in 1830 (having far exceeded the average life of a wooden warship in that time period), poet Oliver Wendell Holmes published his poem "Old Ironsides" in the *Boston Advertiser* on September 30, 1830, and a national outcry resulted in a success. The *Constitution* thereafter was repaired and kept in service, traveling around the world on duty. Finally, in June 1855, her warship duties came to an end when she was decommissioned at Portsmouth, New Hampshire. In subsequent years, *Constitution* was used as a training ship, made one voyage overseas for the Paris Exposition in 1878 and was used again as a training ship until she was designated as being unfit for service in 1881 and was moved to Portsmouth. Here, she was used as a receiving ship at the Portsmouth Naval Shipyard for many years until being towed to Charlestown Navy Yard for centennial celebrations in 1897. Her fate for a number of years after was in doubt, but when, in 1905, the secretary of the navy proposed she be towed out to sea and used for target practice and sunk, a nationwide public campaign soon emerged to not only save the ship but restore her to her former glory. By 1907, she was a museum ship and partially restored, but it was not until 1927 that she entered drydock for a full restoration, with all kinds of publicity surrounding her saving, including the production of a silent movie. The restoration eventually cost nearly $950,000 and took three years. Some 85 percent of the *Constitution* was replaced to make her operational again, but the backbone of the frigate, her live oak keel, remained intact. This remaining component and others kept her a true original. Today, the *Constitution*, which was recommissioned in July 1931, remains moored at Charlestown and has been restored to her War of 1812 configuration, first in 1973–74, just in time for America's Bicentennial, again from 1992 to 1995 and last in 2015–17. On the occasion of her 200th birthday in 1997, the *Constitution* was towed out to sea on July 21 and subsequently sailed under her own sail power for a short time—a glorious sight and the first time in over one hundred years she had done so. Today, moored at the former Charlestown Navy Yard, at the end of the Boston Freedom Trail and adjacent to the USS *Constitution* Museum, she is manned by six officers and about fifty enlisted crew who oversee educational programs and historic events, as well as everyday maintenance and upkeep. The frigate is impeccably maintained and is truly a stunning sight to see. Visitors are able to walk on its main spar deck and talk to its crew.

SARATOGA

There is one theater of the war that we must not forget, and that is the Great Lakes and Lake Champlain, where British naval forces threatened our young country's northern border. The British had suffered a major defeat in September 1813 when they lost control of Lake Erie after Oliver Hazard Perry and his fleet defeated the British at the Battle of Put-in-Bay. However, the British were still determined to invade from the north and turned their eyes toward Lake Champlain between New York and Vermont. Naval dominance of the lake was a key aspect of any plan for invasion, so both sides raced to build a significant fleet. To that end, the navy sent New York City shipbuilder brothers Adam and Noah Brown to Vergennes, Vermont, to build a substantial man-of-war. They were natives of upstate New York and had previously built the Lake Erie fleet. Here, in very quick time, they built the twenty-six-gun corvette *Saratoga* for the American naval commander, Master Commandant Thomas Macdonough. The ship was laid down in early March 1814 and launched just over a month later. She was a well-built vessel and was very heavily sparred. With a crew of 212 men, Macdonough quickly had the *Saratoga* ready for operations and subsequently spent the summer blockading the mouth of the Richelieu River, which flows north from Lake Champlain to the St. Lawrence River. Meanwhile, the British were rushing to complete the thirty-six-gun frigate *Confiance*, the largest warship ever to sail on Lake Champlain. Shore guns served to protect the ship while she was being built up the river at Ile-aux-Noix. While she was completed in late August, Macdonough withdrew his fleet, which also included the fourteen-gun schooner *Ticonderoga*, the newly finished twenty-gun brig *Eagle* and a number of other small vessels, including at least nine small gunboats, into Plattsburgh Bay.

Soon after the British completed *Confiance*, their combined land and naval force was launched in late August, the eight-thousand-strong land army depending on the British fleet for support. On September 11, 1814, the British naval forces rounded Cumberland Head and entered Plattsburgh Bay, the battle underway. The British commander, Captain George Downie in *Confiance*, maneuvered his fleet toward the American line and took heavy fire and, when in range of *Saratoga*, fired a broadside that killed or wounded over forty of her men. Macdonough quickly recovered, and *Saratoga* fired a broadside that killed the British commander. While the battle among the other ships proceeded, *Saratoga* and *Confiance* fought each other to a bloody standstill, with *Confiance*'s fire slowing, while most of *Saratoga*'s starboard-side guns were out of action. However, Macdonough used his kedge anchors to turn his ship around, the port battery being undamaged, and subsequently unleashed a new round of fire. The British ship tried to do the same but was turned only partially and presented her vulnerable stern to the *Saratoga*. Heavily damaged, *Confiance* was forced to strike her colors, after which Macdonough turned *Saratoga* again so that her port guns could be brought to bear on another enemy vessel, the sixteen-gun brig HMS *Linnet*. This vessel, too, was pounded into a sinking condition and was forced to surrender. The battle was soon over after this, with the remaining British vessels retreating.

As for the battle on land, British army forces were ordered to retreat now that their naval supply line was cut, and with that retreat, the final plan to invade the northern United States ended in failure. Following the battle, Thomas Macdonough was promoted to captain. He was hailed as the Hero of Lake Champlain and was later the recipient of a specially commissioned Congressional Gold Medal. His brilliant tactics not only resulted in an American victory that stymied British plans but also had far-

The *Saratoga* (*center*) of Thomas Macdonough hammering the British flagship *Confiance* during the Battle of Lake Champlain, 1814. *Courtesy Naval History and Heritage Command archives.*

ranging implications. The Treaty of Ghent to end the war was then being negotiated, and had the British been victorious on Lake Champlain, our northern border might look very different today. As for the final fate of the *Saratoga*, she was laid up after the war until finally being sold at Whitehall, New York, in 1825. While her final fate is unknown, her name was proudly carried on in the American navy by several ships over the years, including two notable aircraft carriers.

NEXT, WE COME TO the privateers of the War of 1812. As in the American Revolution, these privately armed vessels did significant damage to British merchant shipping, and as historian and former privateer Captain George Coggeshall states, "they were harassing and annoying British trade and commerce wherever a ship could float," including in the Pacific and on their very doorstep off English ports. In all, according to historian Edgar Maclay, 515 privateers were commissioned during the war, including 307 from Massachusetts, 142 from Connecticut, 78 from New Hampshire and 18 from Rhode Island, and all privateers combined captured at least 1,345 vessels and likely many more. Emblematic of this success are the privateers *America* and *Grand Turk* (II) of Salem.

AMERICA

First in importance among these privateers is the *America*, a 350-ton merchant vessel that was built in 1804 and owned by the Crowninshield family of Salem. With a large spread of sail, the *America*, which mounted twenty guns and was manned by 150 men, was said to be the fastest privateer afloat and had a very successful and profitable career. She made her first cruise in 1812 under Captain Joseph Ropes, departing Salem on September 18 and returning in January 1813, having captured six prizes worth $150,000. On her second cruise, which lasted from January to July 1813, she captured ten prizes, while on her third cruise, now under Captain James Chever Jr., she captured twelve prizes while cruising between December 1813 and April 1814. Chever also commanded *America* on her fourth and last cruise, departing for European waters in November 1814 and returning to Salem in April 1815, having her fiercest action of the war when battling an eight-gun British privateer and putting, as historian Maclay states, seven hundred shot holes in her hull, spars and sails. Overall, during the course of the war, *America* brought twenty-seven prizes into port (twenty others were either destroyed or recaptured) carrying cargoes valued at over $1 million. After the war, having seen hard service, *America* lay tied up at the Crowninshields' wharf in Salem for years before finally being sold and scrapped in 1831.

GRAND TURK

Another significant privateer in the War of 1812 from Salem, second only to the *America*, was the *Grand Turk*. This 309-ton, eighteen-gun brig was built as a privateer at Wiscasset, Maine, by Stephen Dutton, being launched in late 1812 and purchased by Salem men. She was not the same vessel as the American Revolution privateer of the same name and was actually the third Salem-owned ship to bear this name. This *Grand Turk* made five cruises during the war and captured thirty vessels, three under Captain Holten

The privateer *Grand Turk*, built at Wiscasset, Maine, in 1812, entering the harbor at Marseilles, France, in 1815. *Courtesy Naval History and Heritage Command archives.*

Breed and the final two under Captain Nathan Green. Under Breed, the *Grand Turk* had a close call in May 1814 when she gave chase to the British West Indies mail packet *Hinchinbroke*, which was armed with nine guns and had a similar crew size. The privateer, which was flying the British Union Jack (an acceptable deception at the time in naval warfare), caught up with the packet after a two-hour chase and quickly lowered the false colors and raised the American flag. Both ships fired their opening broadsides at the same time, after which a fierce battle ensued. The more heavily armed *Grand Turk* twice tried to board the packet, all the while continuing to fire, while the *Hinchinbroke* herself continued to fire. In the end, the ships fought to a draw, the privateer departing with damage and several men killed, while the packet ship had a like number of casualties and was severely damaged. Later on, in March 1815, while cruising off the coast of Brazil, the *Grand Turk* encountered the fourteen-gun brig *Acorn* after a two-hour chase. This time, the outcome was different; while the *Acorn* fired her broadsides first, the *Grand Turk* responded with her port-side battery, the fire so heavy that the English ship surrendered within ten minutes. Following the end of her wartime service, the *Grand Turk* was subsequently sold and operated as a merchant vessel for many years.

WITH THESE TWO VESSELS, we can see the varied life of a successful privateer during the War of 1812 and also the great economic and material loss they inflicted on the British merchant fleet. However, it was also the end of an era. The War of 1812 would be the last war in which American privateers operated in great numbers. The practice of privateering remained legal in America and Europe until the Declaration of Paris was signed by most European nations in 1856, which abolished privateering. Interestingly, the United States did not sign this declaration at first but finally did so in the midst of the Civil War.

Chapter 4

MERCHANT VOYAGERS
AND PACKET SHIPS, 1780–1833

*F*ollowing the end of the American Revolution, and again after the War of 1812, America's shipping trade quickly expanded and sought new growth for trade and prosperity. The shipping trades evolved in two different types of activity: opening and expanding trade to overseas locations in such exotic locales as the East Indies, Hawaii, China, the Mediterranean and the Middle East and that involving the so-called packet, or mail, and passenger trade with European ports. New England seaport towns were known in many instances for the type of trade they conducted. While it was a New York ship that was the first to open the China trade, Boston would soon become a rival in that trade, while just up the coast, Salem became a specialist in the East Indies trade. All of these cities and towns profited from that trade, not just in selling the goods they brought home to America but also in the allied trades, such as shipbuilding, that supported that activity. The expansion of our trade overseas was quite an exciting time in our history. These voyages were often dangerous and groundbreaking, with American ships sailing to exotic places where, in many cases, no American had ever been before. Not only were the cultures and language they encountered something that was totally new, but terrible storms at sea, shipwrecks, piracy and attacks by natives on a hostile shore were not uncommon. This was the ultimate adventure, the American sailor a veritable stranger in a strange land. The period from the 1780s to the 1840s was indeed a whirlwind of trade and exploration, and much of it was carried on in ships built in New England shipyards and crewed by New England sailors and captains. These experiences left an indelible impression on those involved, as is evidenced by looking at a map of Maine, where many sea captains hailed from. Ever wonder why there are so many towns in that state with foreign names, such as China, Peru, Mexico, Norway, Naples, Belgrade, Levant, Canton, Palermo, Denmark, Bremen, Moscow, Sweden and Orient? Chances are, one of the founding fathers was a mariner who had voyaged to that place in person.

EMPRESS OF CHINA

Even before the American Revolution was officially ended, New England–built ships were being sent to far-flung places. While the Treaty of Paris that ended the war was signed in September 1783, it would not be until May 1784 that it was fully ratified. The first ship to fly the American flag in Chinese waters was actually the Boston-built *Empress of China*. This ship, according to her chronicler, Philip Chadwick Foster Smith, was built by John Peck in 1783 and was a square-sterned, full-rigged ship of anywhere between three hundred and five hundred tons (accounts vary), possibly built as a privateer vessel. American merchants were anxious to get to China after the war, and this venture was an elaborate arrangement, first between three parties: principal John Parker, a New York merchant who was a Massachusetts native; a group of Boston merchants; and, most notably, Philadelphian Robert Morris. He was a signer of the Declaration of Independence and, as one of the wealthiest men in America, was known as the "financier of the American Revolution." However, the Boston merchants would eventually withdraw, leaving Parker and Morris to split the venture, leading to some unsavory dealings by Parker. The cargo to China consisted of only two commodities: about $20,000 in Spanish silver coins and just over twenty-five tons of ginseng, an herbal root dug from the ground in forested areas in Virginia and Pennsylvania and shipped to New York over a period of months. These were the only commodities of value that Chinese merchants coveted, especially ginseng, which was widely used as an herbal remedy and cure-all. These commodities, soon enough, would prove to be unsustainable in the China trade, but more about that later.

Commanded by Captain John Green, a former Continental navy officer and a man who had commanded merchant ships for Morris over the years, the *Empress of China* departed New York in February 1784 for China, taking a route that would carry her around the Cape of Good Hope and through

This Chinese five-yuan coin was minted in 1986 to commemorate the 200th anniversary voyage of the pioneer trader *Empress of China*. *Author's collection.*

the Indian Ocean. The voyage took six months with no major problems. The ship arrived in late August and, as was customary in the region, took a pilot at Macao, a Portuguese colony, and also there gained a pass that would allow them admittance for trade. The pilot guided the *Empress of China* up the Canton River before anchoring at Whampoa Roads off Canton (modern-day Guangzhou). Once there, the Americans spent four months learning the ins and outs of dealing with local businessmen, known as hong merchants, and made out fairly well, even though the market for ginseng had dropped considerably. As for a return cargo, the *Empress of China* returned with those items that we traditionally associate with China even today: tea, porcelain-ware, valuable silk and nankeen fabrics. The ship departed China in late December 1784 and made a quick passage home, arriving at New York in early May 1785.

Her arrival and the cargo she carried made immediate news in New York, followed shortly thereafter by publicity in Philadelphia, where Robert Morris would sell his share of the cargo. This one voyage opened the floodgates for the China trade, and the *Empress of China*, now under new ownership, would make a return voyage to China in 1786, even though it was evident that even larger ships for this trade would soon be required. Following her second voyage, the *Empress* was sold yet again and, as historian Smith recounts, was scheduled to make another China voyage but was so damaged by an intermediate trip to France that those plans were scrapped. The ship would eventually be sold yet again, her name changed to *Clara*, and in early 1791, she was wrecked off the coast of Dublin, Ireland. The career of the *Empress of China* was a short one, it is true, but the China trade that she pioneered remains important to this day.

ONE OF THE POTENTIAL investors with Robert Morris in that first China voyage was an adventurous man named John Ledyard. He was a Connecticut native who briefly attended Dartmouth College in New Hampshire and, after dropping out of college in 1773, sought a career as a mariner. In 1776, he served as a sailor in Captain James Cook's third and final voyage of exploration and discovery, which lasted for four years. This voyage touched the Pacific Northwest coast, as well as Alaska, the Aleutian Islands and subsequently Hawaii (where Cook was killed) and the Dutch East Indies and the Portuguese colony at Macao on the China coast. Ledyard noticed that the sea otter fur trade, which animals were acquired all along the Northwest coast from Oregon to Alaska by British traders, was a highly lucrative one, the furs a valuable commodity in China. Upon returning to Dartmouth in 1780, he published in 1784 the journal of his travels with Captain Cook, and it created a great sensation. Ledyard was convinced that the sea otter fur trade would provide reliable trade goods for the China trade and even proposed a partnership with Robert Morris. However, no American ship had even voyaged to the Pacific Northwest, and Morris subsequently went in another direction. Boston merchant Joseph Barrell, having read the journal of Ledyard's travels, was convinced of the feasibility of such a trade and formed a syndicate to pioneer the fur trade in the Northwest, with the intent to trade these furs in China for tea, porcelain, silk and other commodities. He chose an experienced privateer commander of the American Revolution, Captain John Kendrick, as the leader of the expedition, and another privateersman, Captain Robert Gray of Rhode Island, as his second in command.

COLUMBIA AND LADY WASHINGTON

The lead vessel in Barrell's expedition was the *Columbia*, a ship of just over two hundred tons, built in 1773 by the well-known builder James Briggs at Hobart's Landing on the North River in Scituate, Massachusetts. Her name signifying the female personification of the new United States of America was a popular one at the time and particularly appropriate for such an ambitious undertaking. The ship was thoroughly overhauled prior to the 1787 voyage, while another vessel, the ninety-ton brig *Lady Washington*, also took part, commanded by Gray. Little is known about this vessel. The forthcoming voyage would prove beyond a doubt that the *Lady Washington* was a faster vessel than the *Columbia* and easier to handle. The only contemporary images of both ships are also, interestingly enough, found on the commemorative coins, minted in pewter and silver versions, that were produced by Barrell and were meant to be given to some of the expedition's backers, as well as to the Natives in the Pacific Northwest as tokens of friendship. The coin is thought to have been the first ever minted in the United States.

The coin issued to commemorate the Pacific Northwest expedition of the *Columbia* and *Lady Washington*. *From Briggs's* History of Shipbuilding on the North River, *1889.*

The two-ship fleet, manned by a total of forty men, departed Boston on October 1, 1787, the *Columbia* heavily laden with trade goods meant to appeal to the Natives of the Pacific Northwest, including beads, mirrors, fabric, knives, bar iron and other knickknacks. What happened during the three-year odyssey that ensued was a potent mix of international intrigue, exploration and discovery and difficult, and at times shady, business dealings. The first part of the voyage was beset with personnel clashes among the *Columbia*'s crew, as well as the fact that the cargo had been improperly loaded and the ship did not handle well. Stops were made at the Cape Verde Islands and, prior to rounding Cape Horn, the Falkland Islands to repair storm damage to *Columbia*. The two ships became separated while trying to round Cape Horn, with the result that Captain Gray in the *Lady Washington* rounded the Horn first, the first American ship ever to do so, and continued up the South American coast after stopping briefly at one of the Juan Fernandez Islands to see if *Columbia* was nearby. Not seeing their compatriot, Captain Gray forged ahead on his own, arriving in the Pacific Northwest at the mouth of the Klamath River in early August 1788. Proceeding farther north to Tillamook Bay, the crew traded with Natives and went ashore to gather water and wood, but while attempting to depart, they became grounded on a reef. Crewmen were again sent ashore, but this time a fight with the Natives ensued, with one crewman of the *Lady Washington* killed. Previously, Captain Kendrick's orders for the expedition were that the Natives were to be treated well, so this was an inauspicious start to their attempts to start the sea otter fur trade. Captain Gray guided his ship farther up the Pacific coast to Nootka Sound, off Vancouver Island, and there found several British ships.

Six days later, on September 22, 1788, Captain Kendrick and the *Columbia* arrived in Nootka Sound. His voyage up the coast from Cape Horn had been trouble-filled to say the least. Despite orders from Joseph Barrell to avoid any Spanish possessions for fear his ships might be seized, Kendrick headed straight for them after *Columbia* was battered while rounding Cape Horn, putting into Mas a Tierra (now Robinson Crusoe Island) off the Chilean coast, badly in need of repairs and provisions. The kindly Spanish governor allowed Kendrick and his weary crew to come into safe harbor, creating a furor when word reached the viceroy of Peru, who demanded that the foreign ship be seized, as was allowed for in Spanish law. After leaving Mas a Tierra, *Columbia* was pursued by Spanish warships but had gained a nice head-start, and Kendrick avoided capture before arriving in the Pacific Northwest. Within months, Kendrick established good relations with the Natives and was able to control the area fur trade. In July 1789, the *Columbia* and *Lady Washington* departed Nootka Sound, and within days, Gray and Kendrick exchanged commands; Kendrick in *Lady Washington* would stay in the Pacific Northwest to continue the fur trade, the smaller vessel being much easier to maneuver in and among the numerous bays and sounds. Neither Kendrick nor his command would ever return to Boston. Captain Gray, now in command of *Columbia*, departed for Canton, China, her hold filled with some 1,200 furs, stopping en route at the Hawaiian Islands, where two Natives were subsequently taken aboard and, eventually, returned to Boston on *Columbia*. Gray arrived at Canton in early 1790 and traded his furs for tea, some of it deemed to be of a low grade. Not only were there American ships already in Canton, but there were also some shady dealings here on Gray's part. While Gray and *Columbia* were in Canton, Captain Kendrick and *Lady Washington* showed up in Macao but had difficulty getting passage to Canton. The two captains communicated by letter, but their relations by this time were severely strained, and the two never did meet up.

After several months, Gray and *Columbia* departed for Boston and, after having taken the Cape of Good Hope route, arrived back home in early August 1790, thus becoming the first American ship ever to circumnavigate the globe. Not only were her captain and crew hailed as heroes upon their arrival, but the landing of the Hawaiian Island Natives also created a sensation. For the *Columbia*, however, the story does not end here.

Under command of Captain Gray once again, she departed Boston in September 1790 for another voyage to the Pacific Northwest, reaching

Nootka Sound in June 1791. While here, Gray met Kendrick again, and trading activities commenced, though Gray seems to have been particularly hostile toward the Natives and in a number of incidents destroyed several villages and killed many of the Natives. In 1792, while voyaging off the coast of modern-day Oregon and Washington, Gray spotted what looked to be a large river and in April even met up with British explorer Captain George Vancouver in HMS *Discovery*. The two discussed the coast and the possibility of such a river, but Vancouver did not believe there was a river in that location, so Gray, undeterred, continued on alone. On May 11, 1792, he discovered the mouth of a large river—as it turns out, the largest in the Pacific Northwest. He sailed his ship about thirteen miles up the river, naming the river Columbia after his command. Gray's discovery and exploration of the Columbia River would later be the basis for America's claim to the Oregon Territory. As on his first voyage, Gray took *Columbia* from the Pacific Northwest to the Hawaiian Islands and thence to China and back to Boston in July 1793, the first American to twice circumnavigate the globe.

A period lithograph featuring the Massachusetts-built *Columbia* experiencing heavy weather near the mouth of the Columbia River. *Courtesy of the Oregon Historical Society.*

The final fate of the *Columbia* is uncertain, but she seems to have continued in the merchant trade for a number of years before being scrapped. However, not only does her name live on in the Columbia River, but it was also taken by the NASA space shuttle *Columbia* and, since 1958, by the replica sailing ship *Columbia*, built at the Todd Shipyards in Los Angeles, that is still a major attraction at Disneyland in Anaheim, California. As for the *Lady Washington*, she continued in the Pacific Northwest–China trade under Kendrick's command and was an early pioneer in the Hawaiian trade until his death under suspicious circumstances there in December 1794. Afterward, Kendrick's second in command took command and ownership of the *Lady Washington* and sailed her between Macao and the Pacific Northwest for several years. She was finally wrecked on the island of Luzon in the Philippines in July 1797. This pioneer ship, like *Columbia*, lives on today in the form of a replica vessel that was built at Aberdeen, Washington, from 1987 to 1989 and now serves as Washington State's Tall Ship Ambassador, making cruises up and down the Pacific coast.

Union

Close on the heels of the *Columbia*, another voyage to the Pacific Northwest was taken by a Rhode Island crew beginning in late summer 1794. The notable features of this voyage are not simply the fact that it was a voyage to the Pacific, for many other vessels soon joined in this trade; it was the captain himself and his vessel that draw the historian's attention. Samuel Eliot Morison stated that it was "the most remarkable youthful exploit in this bright dawn of Pacific adventure that has come to my notice." The youth in this case was Captain John Boit Jr. of Rhode Island. He had previously served in the crew of *Columbia* at the age of fifteen and thus had already voyaged around the world once. However, several years later, at the age of nineteen, he was given command of the eighty-nine-ton sloop *Union*, which brings us to the second aspect of this voyage. The *Union* was a small vessel, a type that had only one mast and was but sixty feet long. Vessels of this type were handy, especially in coastal exploration, but were seldom meant for long-distance voyaging. Nonetheless, Boit and his twenty-two-man crew, armed with eighteen guns and a full cargo, glided out of Newport in August 1794 for the Pacific Northwest, arriving there the following May after a voyage of 260 days. There, the young captain was

The sloop *Union* made an around-the-world voyage under nineteen-year old Captain John Boit Jr. in 1794–96. *From Morison's* Maritime History of Massachusetts, *1921.*

remembered by the Natives, who well recalled the crew of the *Columbia*, and though his sloop was attacked at one point by hostile Natives (some of whom had turned unfriendly after being mistreated and cheated by British and American fur traders), he ably defended the *Union*. After five months of gathering a fur cargo, Boit headed his command toward Canton by way of a stopover in Hawaii and subsequently arrived at Whampoa Roads in December 1795. There, the youthful captain exchanged his cargo for silk and other commodities and thence departed China for Boston in January 1796 with seven other ships, all of them larger. The voyage home of the *Union* was filled with many events, the most dire being when she nearly lost her mast near the island of Madagascar. However, Captain Boit was able to effect repairs at sea and continued onward, surviving stormy seas, an encounter with a French warship and even being fired on by a British warship on her approach to Boston Harbor. He made port in July 1796 ahead of most of the ships he had sailed with. This remarkable around-the-world voyage was, at the time, the first ever by a sloop-rigged vessel, according to Morison.

RAJAH

If you can recall your school days, you may remember that it was the search for valuable spices that drove exploration in the New World. Christopher Columbus himself was looking for a route to the Far East so that the valuable spice trade, among other things, could be exploited; so were Ferdinand Magellan and many other pioneering European explorers. By the time America was permanently colonized in the first decades of the 1600s, the Dutch controlled the spice trade with their colonies in the East Indies (Indonesia), and it was they who supplied New Englanders with this commodity, pepper being the most important. However, it was not until over one hundred years later that Americans would be directly involved in the pepper trade and cut out the middleman. The man to achieve this was Captain Jonathan Carnes of Salem, a notable privateersman of the American Revolution. After the war, Captain Carnes was employed by the noted Salem merchant Elias Hasket Derby (the owner of the *Grand Turk*), commanding his ship *Grand Sachem*. While in the Far East at the British trading post on the island of Sumatra, Carnes heard a rumor that wild pepper was growing on the coast and was there for the taking, outside control of the Dutch East Indies Company.

While his ship was wrecked off Bermuda during his homeward-bound voyage, Captain Carnes made it home and, armed with his secret knowledge of wild Sumatran pepper, parted ways with his old employer. Intending to undertake a pioneering voyage, he joined with Salem merchant Jonathan Peele, with whom he had already had dealings during the Revolution. The two men built a 130-ton schooner, the *Rajah*, and, armed with four guns and a ten-man crew, departed Salem for Sumatra in November 1795, carrying a cargo of trading goods that included iron, dried fish, brandy and gin. By the time of her departure, news of the voyage had become public, and the hopes for success were not high. Some, according to historian W.A. Fairburn, called it a "damn fool voyage." Without charts or navigation aids of any kind, Captain Carnes made his way through unknown waters to the Sumatran coast and was gone for eighteen months. When he arrived back at Salem in the spring of 1797, he brought back "a cargo of wild pepper in bulk—the first ever imported into America." The cargo cost $18,000 overall to procure but brought in a profit of 700 percent, according to historian Ralph Paine, a vast fortune that made Salem "pepper mad" and resulted in that already prosperous seaport becoming the premier pepper trading location in North America and one of the most important in the world. Captain Carnes would take *Rajah* back to Sumatra for a second profitable voyage, and the die was cast. The pepper trade would remain a staple in Salem until it finally ran its course in the 1850s, the last pepper voyage being made in 1860.

RECOVERY

Americans are obsessed with coffee, now more than ever. So, how did that obsession get started? While the Far East occupied the thoughts of New England merchants in the last decade of the eighteenth century, other parts of the globe were far from being ignored, and it won't be a surprise by now that Salem, Massachusetts mariners and merchants were in the forefront. Coffee wasn't unknown in America prior to 1800, but it was expensive, as it was only previously acquired through trade with the British, who went to the original source well before American ships had voyaged that far. Today, coffee beans are grown and harvested all over the world, including in Africa and closer to home in such South American countries as Colombia. However, did you ever wonder why coffee is also called "mocha"? That's because coffee beans were first imported from Mocha in Yemen, a far-off country located on the Arabian Peninsula, where the coffee arabica plant was grown and a place where no American ship had ever gone before. In fact, the first to do so was the 284-ton ship *Recovery*, built at Salem in 1794 by the famed local builder Retire Beckett for Elias Hasket Derby. Commanded by Captain Joseph Ropes, the *Recovery* departed Salem for Mocha, Arabia, in April 1798, loaded with $50,000 in gold and silver coins. She arrived at her destination in early September. *Recovery* was the first American ship to fly the Stars and Stripes in the region and the first American vessel ever to sail the Red Sea, and she caused a sensation. Local Muslim leaders "could not divine from whence she came" and repeatedly asked "how many moons she had been coming," according to Salem historians Charles Osgood and Henry Batchelder. The Arabian merchants were very willing to deal with these newly arrived foreigners, for Ropes and his crew loaded over 300,000 pounds of coffee beans. They arrived back at Salem in October 1801 and, of course, created a huge demand for mocha that has not diminished to this day. By 1805, Salem ships were importing some 2 million pounds of coffee a year.

NEXT, WE TURN OUR attention to the packet ships. With American merchants, especially New Englanders and New Yorkers, doing more and more business with European traders, as well as the growing shipping volume between various American ports, it soon became the case after the end of the War of 1812 that more regular service was needed between important port cities to accommodate both passengers and timely documents like newspapers and mail (termed "packets" in the day). Prior to 1818 in America, both passengers and mail were carried on an irregular basis. Ships did not sail on a time schedule but only when their holds were fully loaded, which resulted in delays for passengers, while mail and newspapers were only carried on an incidental basis. The idea of a regular service in vessels known as "packet ships" got its start in 1818 when the Black Ball Line was established, operating between the ports of New York and Liverpool, England, as the first ever transatlantic service. Ships departed port on a set day and time (once a month at first, later more frequently), whether their cargo holds and passenger cabins were full or empty. This line, which first utilized New York–built ships, became so popular that within a few years, rival lines would be established. While it must be said that New York shipbuilders were predominant in the packet trade, a number of notable New England–built vessels were also used. Boston built some important early packets, while Newburyport was also a leader for many years. However, in terms of sheer numbers, the state of Connecticut was the leader in New England when it came to building packet ships. The easterly route from America to Europe was always the shortest in terms of time due to prevailing winds and currents, but the westbound run from England back to America was a challenging one for the same reasons of contrary currents. The eastbound route in a fast ship could be as short as the record time of thirteen days and some hours, while the best westbound passage ever took seventeen days, though the average for most ships was somewhat longer of course. The packet lines continued to be profitable for many years, with many lines earning hefty fees from government contracts to carry mail, but by the 1870s, sailing ships were largely pushed out of the trade by steamships, whose day would only come to pass with the advent of transatlantic air travel in the twentieth century.

EMERALD

The 359-ton ship *Emerald* was one of the four ships of Boston's first transatlantic service, the Boston and Liverpool Packet Company, often called the Jewel Line, as each of their four ships was named after a precious stone. The vessel was built in 1822 by John Wade of Boston and was very loftily

The Jewel Line packet ship *Emerald*, built in Boston in 1822. *From Morison's* Maritime History of Massachusetts, *1921.*

sparred, carrying a great spread of canvas given her size. Her commander was Captain Phillip Fox, a native of Cohasset, who was known as a hard driver. This line only lasted for a few years, but during that time, the *Emerald* set a speed record for the run from Liverpool to Boston when in February–March 1824 she made the run in just seventeen days. Her passage was so quick that her owners believed she had not even yet made Liverpool on the outward run and was just returning due to some problem. Luckily, Captain Fox had newspapers from Liverpool to prove his feat. Sadly, the Boston line could not compete with the Black Ball and other lines and folded later that year. *Emerald* would later go on to serve in the merchant service, making voyages to India and elsewhere, but returned to packet service for a brief time in 1846 on a line that ran from Baltimore to Liverpool. The *Emerald* was indeed an important harbinger of things to come in the 1850s, when speed, obtained by hard-driving captains, was supremely important.

SYLVIE DE GRASSE

American packet lines to Le Havre, France, were started in 1822, and this ship, built just over a decade later, would be one of the star performers.

Today, few think of Hartford, Connecticut, as a major seaport, but once upon a time, it was an important maritime center. It is interesting, as historian W.A. Fairburn notes, that the size of the packet ships built on this river had no relation to their distance from the ocean, as it was mostly small coastal packet ships that were built in such towns as Saybrook, while much farther up the river larger oceangoing packets were built. One of the most famous of these was the 641-ton *Sylvie de Grasse*, built in 1833 by D. & H. Burgess at Hartford for New York owners. This ship ran in the Old Havre Line and later the Union Line to the same destination and was known for being a well-built and sturdy vessel. She made good westward passages home, with one incredibly fast 20-day crossing to her credit. Ships like this not only continued the fine tradition of shipbuilding on the Connecticut River, but their quality also made the area a destination for New York merchants looking for a good ship at a price less costly than New York builders could provide. The *Sylvie de Grasse* continued in her packet duties for many years, but when the California Gold Rush began, her owner, William Gray, sent her to California, carrying U.S. Army troops there by government contract. She departed New York in November 1848 and arrived in San Francisco in April 1849, 149 days later, two weeks of which were spent in port at Valparaiso, Chile. Not a bad time at all. From there, Gray subsequently voyaged to the Oregon coast to load timber up the Columbia River to bring back to San Francisco. This lumber was in high demand for the rapid building that was taking place due to the large influx of gold-seekers. However, *Sylvie de Grasse* would never make it back. While waiting for a pilot to guide her out to sea, the vessel drifted onto some rocks, where her lumber cargo subsequently shifted, leaving her wedged in place. Despite efforts to free the old packet ship, it was not to be, and here would be her final resting place. Even twenty years later, her hulk, with her once beautiful figurehead now headless, still marked the spot, and as late as 1895, the remains of this once celebrated Connecticut-built packet ship were still highly visible at the mouth of the Columbia at low tide.

Chapter 5

WHALING AND FISHING VESSELS, 1799–1926

The activities of those who harvest the bounty of the sea represent one of the oldest and longest-lasting economic pursuits in America, including three different areas that apply here, that of the fisheries of the North Atlantic, the whalers and those engaged in the sealing trade.

Once the English colonies were established in Virginia, Massachusetts, New Hampshire and elsewhere, cod fishing in the cold waters of the North Atlantic soon became not only vitally important in feeding the colonists but, as larger vessels were built, larger catches also resulted in a valuable trading commodity. This included dried and salted fish that was first exported to England as foodstuffs but soon enough was sent to the West Indies to feed the slaves who were brought there from Africa, a vital component in the triangular trade. Cod fishing was so important in Massachusetts that a wooden likeness of the fish was on display in the statehouse for many years, while cod-themed weathervanes flew above the meetinghouses of many seaport towns, including Marblehead and Gloucester. Even after the end of the triangular trade, cod-fishing remained a vital part of the New England economy for years, going into a decline only after World War II, when larger and more powerful fishing vessels with bigger nets and on-board refrigeration units soon led to a decrease. Of course, cod was not the only type of fish to be caught, with haddock and halibut being mainstays, as well as the transportation of frozen herring (in barrels) from Newfoundland to processing plants in Gloucester. For the fishery trade, a good, solid vessel was needed, one that could well handle the harsh conditions of the North Atlantic but also had a turn of speed, able to get a fisherman's catch home in good time in the days before refrigeration. This vessel turned out to be the fishing schooner, which typically had two masts and had a fore-and-aft ("front to back") rig, where the sails run along the line of the keel. This type was popular in America by the early 1700s, with both Baltimore and Marblehead vying for its invention, according to folklore and long-held traditions. No matter how it came to be, the schooner would be a mainstay in the fisheries from the 1700s until the end of the age of sail, with many such vessels still in operation into the twentieth century. Many ports were involved in the trade.

It was Gloucester, Massachusetts, which began building its own fishing boats in the early 1700s, that emerged as the first and dominant fishing port of New England (and the nation), maintaining that status for over two hundred years. Today, it is second only to New Bedford in New England, while Massachusetts is second in terms of the value of the fishing industry nationwide, with Alaska being the leader. However, despite these modern changes, Gloucester today remains a true fishing port. You can see that heritage all around you, and not just in the many commercial wharves and modern fishing boats. Here you can also see the monuments dedicated to those who took part in the fisheries, including the famed Gloucester Fisherman's Memorial, the Gloucester Fishermen's Wives Memorial and the large memorial in city hall dedicated to Gloucester fishermen lost at sea. As to the trade itself, the fishing schooners voyaged from their home ports, first to Georges Bank, just over sixty miles off the Massachusetts coast, but later farther afield to the Grand Banks off Newfoundland, a spot where two ocean currents meet: the cold Labrador Current from the north and the Gulf Stream Current from the south. This merging of two currents roils the waters, which, along with the relatively shallow waters, brings nutrients to the surface and makes for excellent feeding ground for fish and seabirds alike. These factors made the Grand Banks one of the richest fishing grounds in the world until it was finally closed in 1992 due to overfishing. The fishermen made their catches by two methods—first by hand off the fishing boats themselves, with each fisherman handling a line that was hundreds of feet long with two hooks, and later by the 1850s, fishermen were fishing the grounds from small boats called dories, which measured about eighteen feet long and could hold two men and up to a ton of fish. These craft were transported to the fishing banks on the decks of a fishing schooner, their shape allowing them to be nestled on top of each other. The dorymen handled lines that were a mile or more long and carried hundreds of hooks. Their job was to row the dory along these lines and bring in the fish that had been hooked, many six feet long. It was tough and back-breaking work on its own, not made any easier by rough seas and stormy weather. One other hazard was being lost in the fog created by the merging of warm and cold ocean currents, with many a doryman being lost in the fog and never seen again.

Effie M. Morrissey
(Now the *Ernestina-Morrissey*)

This schooner is one of the most famous fishing vessels in the world. The 120-ton *Effie M. Morrissey*, named after Captain William Morrissey's daughter, was built at the shipyard of John James and Washington Tarr in nearby Essex (some sources state her builder as Willard Burnham) and launched in 1894. The *Morrissey* was built for John Wonson & Company and Captain Morrissey. The Wonsons were then the owner of seventeen fishing schooners and known for pioneering the winter halibut fishery on Georges Bank. The schooner was successful from the start, even making several voyages under Captain Morrissey's nineteen-year-old son. During the Portland Gale of 1898, the *Morrissey* went ashore after tearing away from her mooring at Wonton's wharf but was refloated with but little damage. In 1905, with sailing schooners on the decline in the fishing industry, the *Morrissey* was sold to owners in Nova Scotia. Though sailing with a Canadian crew, she remained registered as an American vessel and landed her catches both in Gloucester and Portland, Maine. In 1914, the *Effie M. Morrissey* was sold yet again, this time going under Newfoundland ownership and British registry. While under the subsequent ownership of Captain Robert Bartlett beginning in 1926, the hull of the schooner was specially sheathed, and a diesel engine was installed for cruising to Greenland and Arctic waters. Bartlett was previously known for taking part in the 1908 Peary Expedition to discover the North Pole, and while in command of the *Morrissey* from 1926 to 1944, he made numerous expeditionary voyages to the Arctic on behalf of American museums and the National Geographic Society and even helped survey the region for the U.S. government during World War II, voyaging as far as Murmansk, Russia. During this time, the *Morrissey* was famed throughout the world for her voyages.

By 1945, the *Effie M. Morrissey* was back in Gloucester, and after the death of Captain Bartlett in 1946, she was sold to New York owners and used as a common freighter until she caught fire and sank at Flushing, New York, in 1947. However, this was not the end for the venerable ship.

The Gloucester fishing schooner *Effie M. Morrissey* as she appeared circa 1894. *From Thomas's* Fast and Able, *1952.*

Refloated, repaired and her engine removed, she was sold to Captain Henrique Mendes and his sister Louise Mendes of New Bedford, who renamed her *Ernestina* after the captain's daughter and put her in the packet trade between that city and the Cape Verde Islands beginning in 1948. Many Cape Verdeans, including the Mendes family, immigrated to New England and made the old whaling port their home, so the packet trade served as a way for these immigrants to keep in touch with their homeland. For the next ten years, the ship carried cargo and passengers between Cape Verde and New England, and it is notable for being the last sailing ship to carry immigrants to America. The *Ernestina* went out of service on the New England run in 1959 and was afterward sold for use to sail among the Cape Verde Islands from 1967 to 1975.

With Cape Verde gaining its independence from Portugal in 1975, their government hoped to sail her back to America to take part in Operation Sail 76 and the parade of Tall Ships that was to take place in New York. However, the old schooner was dismasted while attempting to cross the Atlantic and returned to Cape Verde, where she was subsequently repaired, restored and presented to the Commonwealth of Massachusetts as a gift from the Cape Verdean people. In 1982, she sailed to the United States with a Cape Verdean and American crew. The schooner, now renamed *Ernestina-Morrissey* and homeported in New Bedford, subsequently took part in Operation Sail 86 and was designated a National Historic Landmark in 1990. Since 2016, the *Ernestina-Morrissey* has been undergoing restoration work in Boothbay Harbor, Maine.

ADVENTURE

The 130-ton knockabout schooner *Adventure* was built in 1926 at the Essex shipyard of Everett James and is an important vessel for several reasons. Not only is she a survivor in sail to this day, but she is also an example of an important type of schooner that evolved specifically due to the dangers involved in the fishing trade. The "knockabout" schooner was designed by Thomas McManus, a man who began his career as a fish dealer but by the 1880s was designing his own fishing schooners, influenced by his fisherman friends. The important change incorporated in the design of the knockabout was the lack of a bowsprit and the extended bow of the vessel. The bowsprit is a long spar extending from the bow of a ship, to which is attached the forestays, which are standing rigging helping to keep the foremast of a vessel from toppling over during times of great stress. On those vessels so rigged, sailors were often required to stand on the bowsprit to make adjustments, exposed to the fullest of the ocean's dangers, and many a man was swept overboard and lost, especially on the fishing schooners that operated in all kinds of weather. McManus's design was one that would save an untold number of lives. As to the ship's career, it was written by Gordon W. Thomas, the man who named her, that "the fame of the *Adventure* is genuine, not gained through publicity as a racer or showboat but through hard, long years on the banks battling storms and hard weather, piling up tremendous stocks year after year."

The vessel was built by a group of businessmen and fishermen of Gloucester, led by Captain Jeffrey Thomas, by then a well-known and successful fishing captain who had commanded at least ten fishing schooners prior to this venture. Captain Thomas's son, Gordon W. Thomas, was a youth at the time who liked to draw pictures of fishing schooners with "imaginary names." When it came time to name his new vessel, Captain Thomas took a look at his son's drawings, hoping to find an inspiration. One of the names his son had used was *Adventure*, and so that became the name of the new schooner. The schooner was 107 feet long, equipped with an auxiliary diesel engine, and was one of the last of her kind built at Essex, with only two schooners built after her. Right from the start, the *Adventure* and her crew were successful in the fishing business, with Captain Thomas taking in many notable hauls, including 100,000 pounds of halibut worth nearly $12,000 in the fall of 1927. The schooner also had her share of hardships and death; she went ashore at Sheet Harbor, Nova Scotia, after striking White Shoal and developing a severe leak, while in 1934 Captain Jeffrey Thomas died

The "knockabout" schooner *Adventure*, built in Essex, Massachusetts, in 1926 and still afloat today as a museum ship. *From Thomas's* Fast and Able, *1952*.

of a heart attack while sailing off Halifax. Command of the schooner was subsequently taken over by Captain Leo Hynes of Boston, who "smashed all records in the fisheries" but also had his share of mishaps. In 1939, the *Adventure* was hit by a large wave, which swept two men overboard to drown, while in 1943, strangely enough, she rammed and sank the *Adventure II*, a schooner named after her and with the same owner, in a dense fog in Boston Harbor. However, it was Hynes's skill as a "dory trawler" that brought *Adventure* fame and her owners fortune in the fishing world, with her landing over $3 million in stock from 1934 to 1953. When her fishing career ended in 1953, she was the last of the dory fishing schooners, thus closing a chapter in the history of the fisheries that had lasted for one hundred years.

Following this, the *Adventure* was sold to an owner in Portland, Maine, for use in the windjammer business, carrying passengers in the summer season off the Maine coast, and in 1965 she was sold again, this time to Captain James Sharp of Camden, Maine, who continued her in the windjammer trade. In 1988, he donated the *Adventure* to the people of Gloucester, and from that time until 2015, she underwent expensive repairs and restoration. The work was halted for much of this time until sufficient funds could be raised.

However, since 2015 she has returned to active sailing and has served as a center for maritime educational programs, as well as a "living monument" to Gloucester fishermen.

WHILE THE FISHERIES WERE a part of New England life from the very beginning, the business of whaling was not far behind. The first purpose-built whaleships were built on the island of Nantucket by the first decade of the 1700s, the Quaker population there becoming the dominating force in the trade. The vessels at first were small ships or barks, no more than fifty tons, the only difference among them being that a ship-rigged vessel used square sails on all three masts, while a bark-rigged vessel utilized square sails on the fore and mainmasts and the mizzenmast (the mast at the stern) used triangular-shaped fore-and-aft sails. The bark was generally considered an easier vessel to handle and one that was more economical, requiring fewer crew members to operate. By the 1850s, whaling vessels averaged between three hundred and four hundred tons. As for the hull of a whaling ship, it was not designed for speed but more for carrying capacity and stability, so it had a bluff and rounded bow and a square stern and was a "beamy," or wide, vessel overall. The whaleship, in fact, was a factory ship, upon whose deck whale carcasses were processed for their bone and oil, the final product being stored in barrels below deck. The whaleship was seldom described as a "pretty" vessel and was not going to turn any heads in port or outrace any but another whaleship at sea. Whaling voyages at first took part in Atlantic waters, with Nantucket being the primary port, but as whaling ships got larger and could not cross the sandbar at the entrance to the harbor, mainland New Bedford would eventually become the leader as the industry grew. Other Massachusetts coastal towns also sent ships out. Many other ports in New England and New York also sent out whalers, with New London being the largest whaling port outside of Massachusetts.

The early whaling voyages were conducted relatively close to home but gradually expanded, with whalers reaching the Davis Strait off Greenland to the north by the 1730s, the coast of Africa by the 1760s and the Falkland Islands by the 1770s. The first American whaling ship would not round Cape Horn into the Pacific until 1791 and first worked the waters off Chile before expanding northward and west toward Hawaii, touching there in 1819 before moving even farther afield to the rich whaling grounds between Japan and Hawaii. Many whaling voyages lasted three or four years, and seldom did a whaler return to New England in less time unless her master had no luck in finding whales. Those whalers that made a good haul were said to have had "greasy luck." The primary species hunted were right whales in the Atlantic, but once whalers went farther afield to the Pacific, the sperm whale (also called a "cachalot") was their primary target. Crew sizes on whalers varied anywhere from ten to fifteen men on the first and smallest vessels, while on the larger ships and barks in the heyday of whaling up to forty-man crews were common. What is most interesting is that whaling crews represented one of the most diverse workplaces anywhere in the world, including whites, African American and Cape Verdeans, Gay Head Indians from Martha's Vineyard and even Hawaiian Island Natives. The officer ranks were typically white, though African Americans also served in these positions and captained vessels. In addition to captain, first, second and third mates and regular seamen, crews also consisted of boatsteerers/harpooners, blacksmiths, coopers, carpenters, cooks and stewards.

As for the actual capture and processing of a whale, the process went something like this. Once in the cruising grounds where whales could be found, a lookout at the mainmast was employed around the clock to spot whales in the distance, often looking for a whale spouting. When one was spotted, the cry, "Thar she blows!" was made. This was a signal for action. Soon enough, three whaleboats were got into the water, having been transported on deck, each commanded by one of the ship's mates and having men to row the boat toward its prey, as well as the boatsteerer, who also served as a harpooner. Once close to the surfaced whale, it became a game of cat and mouse. Sometimes a whale would become spooked and sound, or it would go deep below the waves while the whaleboat crew had to guess where the whale might resurface. Once a whaleboat was able to make a close approach to the surfaced mammal, the chase became even more dangerous, as one swat of a whale's tail could demolish a wooden boat. The harpooner now stood at the bow of the whaleboat, ready to make his initial strike with expert precision. Attached to the harpoon was a strong rope, many fathoms long, for once wounded, many a whale sounded again or took off on the surface in an attempt to escape. Since one end of the rope was anchored to the whaleboat, such an escape resulted in a "Nantucket sleigh ride," where a whale would pull the whaleboat behind it at speeds approaching twenty-five miles per hour. However, if a crew was successful, the whale would eventually tire, and the whaleboat would move in for the final kill using hand lances and spears to strike at vital regions of the leviathan.

It was a lucrative business to be sure, but it was also a dangerous and bloody one, and not just for the whale. Many a man was lost in a whaleboat that was smashed to pieces or dragged below the waves, or sometimes they even ended up in the mouth of a whale. It was also not uncommon for a man to be yanked overboard tangled in the harpoon rope and dragged below the surface to drown. Whaling, in its day, was one of the most dangerous occupations in America. Once a whale was killed, the work was just beginning. The carcass was then towed back to the ship and hauled alongside, where the masts and yardarms served as derricks to hoist the dead whale out of the water. Then the process of flensing the carcass began, with all crewmen pitching in to peel the skin away and cut the blubber into chunks. Prior to this, brick ovens called "tryworks" had been set up on deck so that the blubber could quickly be put to boil, turned into oil and put up in barrels. It was often remarked that the deck of a whaler, processing a carcass deep into the night, was a vision of Dante's inferno, the flames from the tryworks lighting the sky for miles in unearthly fashion. At the height of this processing, the deck of a whaler was covered in a mixture of blood, gore, blubber and oil and was a disgusting mess. It took a strong stomach indeed to be a whaler, and the approach of a whaler to port could often be foretold by her unique odor. It was a difficult life to serve aboard a whaler, though one that many Americans today perceive as a romantic and adventure-filled one.

Like the fisheries business, the day of the whaler in the age of sail would gradually come to an end. The beginning of the end came when oil was

An old-time whaling scene that dramatizes the all-too-real dangers of everyday life that existed in the whaling industry in the nineteenth century. *From Dow's* Whale Ships and Whaling, *1925.*

discovered at Titusville, Pennsylvania, in 1859. That fossil fuel eventually supplanted whale oil in the energy business. This was followed up during the Civil War, when Confederate raiders decimated the whaling fleets of New England, capturing and destroying huge numbers of New England whaling ships in the Atlantic and Pacific in the hopes of disrupting the North's economy. Though they failed in that aim, in the spring of 1865, the raider CSS *Shenandoah* alone captured twenty New England whalers in the Bering Sea, almost half of the Arctic whaling fleet. The final big blow to the whaling industry came in 1871, when thirty-three of the forty ships engaged in the Arctic whaling trade were trapped and subsequently crushed in the pack ice, an unprecedented disaster that crippled the industry. This was an event from which it never recovered, though whalers would still put out from the primary port of New Bedford for many years after and even into the twentieth century. For many years afterward, however, most surviving whalers lay tied up in New Bedford, slowly rotting at their moorings. Today, only one American whaling ships remains of the hundreds, perhaps thousands, that were used in the trade.

ESSEX

If forced to pick one New England–built ship that is best known to all Americans, the *Essex* would rate high on that list for her place in the annals of American literature. This 238-ton ship was built in 1799, and for many years her origin was unknown, reported to be built either on Nantucket or by a North River builder in Plymouth County, Massachusetts. Recent research has proved that she was actually built at Amesbury on the Merrimack River. Beginning in 1804, she was owned on Nantucket and began her career as a whaler, making five voyages between 1804 and 1819 and considered a lucky ship due to the fact that she usually returned home with a full cargo hold, filled with anywhere from 1,300 to 1,500 barrels (approximately 32 gallons each) of oil. However, by 1819, she was old and small by industry standards.

On August 12, 1819, she departed Nantucket with a twenty-one-man crew under the command of Captain George Pollard Jr. He had previously served aboard the *Essex* from 1815 to 1819 as second and first mate. The newly promoted captain, assisted by his friend and first mate Owen Chase, guided the whaler toward the Pacific. Just two days out, the ship was battered by a sudden squall, which destroyed several of her whaleboats and damaged her rigging, but the ship continued on, arriving off Cape Horn in early December and subsequently taking five weeks to make it around the Horn. Finding the whaling grounds off the coast of Chile depleted, the *Essex* proceeded farther west, heading to grounds several thousand miles off the coast of South America after first stopping at the Galapagos Islands to gather food supplies, including three hundred of the giant tortoises for which the island was known, as well as to make repairs. The ship finally arrived in her chosen hunting grounds in November 1820 but found no whales for weeks, which led to low morale and even some dissention among her officers. The first whale encountered got away, smashing first mate Owen Chase's whaleboat to pieces.

A pod of sperm whales was finally sighted on November 20, and the ship's three remaining whaleboats were dispatched. Chase's whaleboat was again damaged and had to return to *Essex*, while the others, including Captain Pollard's boat, each harpooned their prey and were subsequently taken on a Nantucket sleigh ride, away from their mother ship. Meanwhile, Chase was aboard *Essex* effecting repairs when the crew spotted an eighty-five-foot-long sperm whale. It lay quietly facing the ship, evidently planning an attack, and then began to swim toward *Essex*, gaining speed as it approached, subsequently ramming the ship's side and then diving underneath. It surfaced on the starboard side, apparently stunned by the impact. Though Chase and the crew tried to harpoon the whale, it was lying so close to the ship that it was feared that if further provoked, its thrashing might destroy the ship's rudder. Subsequently regaining its senses, the whale swam several hundred yards away from the *Essex* and then turned and lay facing her bow. Once again, the enraged whale—there is no other way to describe it—swam quickly toward the *Essex*, this time striking the bow with such force that the ship's timbers were crushed. Once the whale disengaged and swam away, never to be seen again by the crew, the old whaler began to sink by the bow. Some navigational equipment was saved from below, and her remaining crew were able to take to the repaired whaleboat before *Essex* sank. Shortly, the ship's other whaleboats arrived on the scene, Captain Pollard stunned by the events. The three whaleboat crews subsequently gathered what floating supplies they could from what remained of the wreck and then, after some disagreement between Pollard and the rest of the crew as to their destination, decided to set a course in their open boats for the South American coast, some two thousand miles distant.

The ordeal of the *Essex* crew was now just beginning. This is a story that has been told numerous times and one that has been strong in the American consciousness ever since the fate of the *Essex* became known to the general public. The subsequent eighty-nine-day odyssey was highlighted by death,

Ship Essex, of Nantucket, having been stove by a whale November, 1820.

Woodcut illustration of the whaling ship *Essex* being stove by a whale. *From Dow's* Whale Ships and Whaling, *1925*.

deliberate murder, cannibalism and, ultimately, the survival of eight of the original twenty survivors. The story told by Owen Chase in his published narrative was enough to make the *Essex* a legend, but it was novelist Herman Melville who gave the ship undying fame, serving as part of his literary inspiration for his great American novel *Moby-Dick*. While Melville had actually served aboard a whaler and gained much of the background for the novel from his direct experiences, the character of Captain Ahab was inspired in part by the *Essex* and Captain George Pollard Jr. This captain was subsequently deemed unlucky. For many years thereafter, he worked in Nantucket as a night watchman, keeping a lonely vigil over the island's wharves and ships, and was both an interesting and haunting figure to Melville. Through Melville's amazing literary work, the story of New England whaling lives on.

GLOBE

This 293-ton whaling ship, built in 1815 by Elisha Foster & Sons on the North River in Scituate for Christopher Mitchell & Co., had a short career as whaling ships go but nonetheless gained fame not only as a pioneer in the trade but also a measure of infamy for the bloody mutiny that marred the last years of her career. The *Globe*'s first whaling voyage began in October 1815 when she departed Nantucket under the command of Captain George

Gardner. The ship returned home on New Year's Day 1818 with 2,015 barrels of whale oil, the first whaleship ever to exceed the 2,000-barrel mark. This was just the beginning. On her second voyage under Gardner (who spent but three months ashore between voyages) from March 1818 to May 1820, she gathered a cargo of 2,090 barrels of sperm oil and, while in the process of doing so, made history. Gardner was the first to discover, as historian Elmo P. Hohman states, "the great Off-Shore Grounds, including hundreds of square miles in mid-Pacific." Gardner's third voyage in the *Globe* was also a moneymaker, netting a cargo of 2,025 barrels of oil while sailing from 1820 to 1822. Gardner, acknowledged as one of Nantucket's most successful whaling captains by this time, subsequently took command of a larger whaler, taking all his luck with him.

Globe's next voyage would be a terrible ordeal. The whaler departed Nantucket for the Pacific under the command of Captain Thomas Worth in December 1822. After filling her holds with whale oil while hunting in the newly discovered grounds off Japan, the ship voyaged to Hawaii, where six of her men promptly deserted, a not uncommon occurrence in this island paradise. Sadly, of the seven new crewmen taken aboard to fill out the *Globe*'s roster, four would be trouble.

Once the whaler departed Hawaii, a mutiny broke out on the ship while near Fanning Island, some nine hundred miles south of Hawaii. The subsequent story of how this mutiny played out has been told in book form many times over the years. The ringleader of the mutiny—not the only one in whaling history but by far the most well known—was Samuel Comstock, who resented the *Globe*'s captain and officers. A special hatred was reserved for third mate Nathaniel Fisher, who had bested Comstock in a seemingly friendly wrestling match aboard the ship, after which a fight ensued, with Fisher soundly thrashing Comstock and the latter then threatening revenge. On the night of January 25–26, 1824, the mutiny erupted, with the officers targeted first. Captain Worth and the first mate were brutally attacked and subsequently murdered while off-duty and asleep, but second mate Lumbert and third mate Fisher fought Comstock, who was armed with two muskets. Fisher nearly had Comstock beaten but was persuaded to surrender to the mutineers who outnumbered them, as Comstock told Fisher that his life would be spared. Upon surrendering, Comstock ran Lumbert through with a bayonet and then shot Fisher in the head after bringing up the wrestling match incident. This was just the beginning of the bloodshed and madness. With the mutineers now in control of the ship—some of the crew participating only so that their lives might be spared—the *Globe* would eventually sail away, but not before a kangaroo court was held by Comstock. He accused one of his own mutineers of plotting to recapture the ship. This man was subsequently found guilty and hanged aboard the ship. In February, the ship finally made Milli Atoll, one of the largest of the Marshall Islands. There, Comstock apparently hoped to set up his own kingdom, but just days after landing, one of the mutineers killed Comstock, after which six of the mutineers sailed away in *Globe*, leaving the remaining nine men stranded on the island. These men did not get along with the Native islanders, with the result that all but two of them were killed. The survivors were finally rescued by a U.S. Navy vessel in 1825. As for the *Globe*, she sailed away under the guidance of Gilbert Smith, eventually making land at Valparaiso, Chile, where the mutineers were taken into custody. The *Globe* finally made it back to Nantucket in November 1824. After this event, the *Globe* would make but one more whaling voyage, this time under Captain Reuben Swain, departing port in June 1825 and returning home with 2,105 barrels of oil in May 1828. After this time, the *Globe* sailed no more as a whaler, perhaps viewed as a cursed ship due to the mutiny and the publicity surrounding it, despite her "greasy luck." She was soon sold to foreign owners in Buenos Aires, and the worn-out vessel was broken up there about 1830. While the legacy of this whaling ship may be viewed as tainted by some, her success as a pioneer under Captain Gardner is significant, while the bloody mutiny itself is part of whaling's colorful lore and legend.

CHARLES W. MORGAN

This historic ship not only had the longest career of any whaler ever to take to the high seas, but she also holds a venerable position as both the oldest merchant vessel afloat and the only remaining example of an American whaling ship. The 351-ton ship was built by Jethro and Zachariah Hillman in New Bedford for her namesake owner and merchant. After fitting out and provisioning, the *Morgan* departed New Bedford on her first voyage in May 1841, commanded by Captain Thomas Norton and headed for the whaling grounds off the coast of Peru. There, the ship had great success, capturing many whales and bringing home a cargo of 1,900 barrels of sperm oil. It was an auspicious start to a career that would last eighty years and consist of thirty-seven voyages, each being anywhere from a year to four years in duration.

After her third voyage ended in 1853, the ship was sold to Isaac Howland Jr. & Co. of New Bedford. This company would own the *Morgan* until about 1863, when she was sold to another well-known New Bedford company owned by J. & W.R. Wing. They would own the *Morgan* for the next fifty years. The whaler was homeported at New Bedford for most of her career, but from late 1887 to 1904, she was homeported in San Francisco. For her first thirty-four whaling voyages, the *Morgan* was primarily hunting her prey in the warm waters of the Pacific, and though she did make some cruises to the North Pacific, she was fortunate to be nowhere near that area when the 1871 whaling fleet met with disaster. After that time, she was part of a slowly diminishing whaling fleet but still survived as a profitable operator, helped in part by the fact that she had been re-rigged as a bark in 1867.

By 1913, the old whaler had been sold to Captain Benjamin Cleveland after one voyage to J.A. Cook of New Bedford. For her final three whaling voyages during the fast-ending age of sail, the *Morgan* made shorter voyages, lasting anywhere from nine to eleven months in the Atlantic waters closer

The 1841-built whaling ship *Charles W. Morgan* under full sail. *From Dow's* Whale Ships and Whaling, *1925.*

to home, likely due to her antiquated condition. On her thirty-seventh and final whaling voyage, she sailed out of Provincetown, returning there in May 1921. Following this, the *Morgan* was moored in New Bedford, one of only two surviving whaleships, the other being the bark *Wanderer*; after this vessel was wrecked in 1924, the *Charles W. Morgan* was the sole survivor. At this point in time, and for some years after, there was little hope or expectation that the *Morgan* would survive. Seeing her slowly decaying, historian Elmo Hohman lamented that the *Morgan* was "venerable but pathetic, never venturing from port, her deserted mast-heads and silent forecastle stand in tragic contrast to the era of world-girdling voyages and oil-soaked decks of which she is the last mute reminder."

Luckily, this would not be how the whaler would end her days. The *Morgan* was nearly destroyed when a steamer in Fairhaven harbor caught fire and drifted down toward the whaler, but local firemen saved the ship. This event spurred on local citizens to think about saving the historic vessel, with the result that local businessman Edward Howland Green, whose ancestors had once owned the *Morgan*, purchased the ship and had her towed to his Round Hill estate in Dartmouth. He founded a nonprofit company called Whaling Enshrined. After restoration was completed in 1926, the whaler was gifted to Whaling Enshrined and put on display, held in a special berth that was constructed for her. This seemed a good solution to saving the ship, but with the death of Green in 1935 and the subsequent lengthy litigation surrounding his estate, the *Morgan* was left in limbo for some years. After the *Morgan* was severely battered by the Hurricane of 1938, Whaling Enshrined tried to get the funds for repairs but could not do so, and once again the whaler was in danger.

A lasting solution came in 1941, when the *Morgan* was acquired by the Marine Historical Society of Mystic, Connecticut, now known as the Mystic Seaport and Museum. The *Charles W. Morgan* was subsequently towed to Mystic after a difficult journey, which involved cutting a channel from her berth to the ocean and one temporary stranding. Once in Connecticut, the *Morgan* became the centerpiece for what would later become Mystic Seaport, with the bark undergoing repairs and being declared a National Historic Landmark in 1966. For many years, the whaler was berthed on dry land, but after repairs in 1968, she took to a floating berth once again but was not seaworthy. However, the folks at Mystic had a vision of getting her back to sea beginning in 2010, when, after much study, it was decided to restore her to seagoing status. In July 2013, the *Morgan* was relaunched, and by June 2014, she was ready to take to the ocean and set her sails once more,

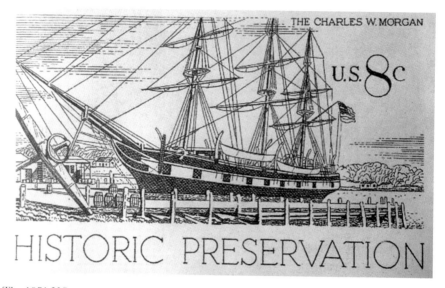

The 1971 U.S. postage stamp featuring the preservation of the whaler *Charles W. Morgan*. *Author's collection.*

departing on her thirty-eighth voyage. Under the command of Captain Kip Files of Rockland, Maine, and a crew of fifteen sailors, as well as a cadre of so-called voyagers—consisting of historians, authors, artists, musicians and performers who enhanced the public experience aboard the whaler— the ship visited several New England seaports during an eight-week cruise. During this time, the *Morgan* was shadowed by a tug and other assisting vessels, as there were real dangers and even the possibility of losing such a historic vessel. She was always towed in and out of ports but did gather sail on her own in the open sea. During her voyage, the *Charles W. Morgan* visited many of her old haunts from one hundred years before, including Newport, Vineyard Haven, Provincetown, her longtime homeport of New Bedford and Boston, and thence back to New London. During the cruise, some right whales were encountered while sailing the Stellwagen Bank off Massachusetts. Could one of these same mammals, when but a young whale, have perhaps encountered the *Morgan* on one of her final voyages in 1920? Possibly so, as whales of this species are known to have a lifespan of up to one hundred years. Today, the *Charles W. Morgan* is tied up at Chubb Wharf, a granite wharf constructed in 1974 that was modeled on her original wharf in New Bedford. The well-cared-for whaler to this day may be seen by visitors, who can walk on her deck like the whaling men of old.

Our final vessel in this chapter about the fisheries concerns the sealing industry. The taking of seals for their meat and fur got its start thousands of years ago when Native tribes like the Inuit in what is now Greenland and Alaska began to hunt for these sea mammals. The English first got involved in the sealing trade on a widespread basis in the late eighteenth century, after the end of the American Revolution, and by the 1790s, American ships became increasingly involved. The commercial seal industry that was developed by the British and Americans was exploitative and unsustainable. Much like whaling, the seals were valued not just for their fur, which was a valuable trading commodity in Europe and the Far East, but also for their blubber, which was melted down for lamp oil and used in processing leather, as well as for their meat. Though sealing is practiced on a limited basis today, the sealing industry even in the early years had long periods when the seals had been hunted to near extinction. For American ships in the age of sail, this industry was only economically viable for less than one hundred years. American merchants and ship owners utilized the seal trade much as Boston merchants did the sea otter trade in the Pacific Northwest, harvesting seals largely just for their fur and then trading these furs in China. One of the prime differences, however, was in the way in which the seal skins were procured. Unlike the sea otter trade, which involved trading for skins harvested by Native peoples, sealing crews actually performed the business of hunting and killing the seals, first on the rocky coast of South America and later on South Georgia Island, located some eight hundred miles south of the Falklands. The business was a gruesome one, where groups of men were employed clubbing the seals to death, dispatching them with a blow to the skull, when they were found resting ashore on beaches or on the rocks. The men would position themselves between the seals and the water to prevent their prey from escaping. In many cases, in just one hunt over one thousand seals would meet their end, the carcasses being skinned of their fur right on the beach and their blubber barreled for transport home. The skins were dried on the rocks along the Argentinian coast. New Haven historian Thomas Trowbridge recounted that New Haven sealers called one section used thus "the New Haven Green." These dried skins were subsequently carried directly to China. Connecticut merchants and shipowners, in particular, were active in this trade, with Stonington being one of the primary ports beginning in the 1790s.

HERO

The forty-ton sloop *Hero* was built in Groton, Connecticut, in 1820. Her building was sponsored by a group of men in nearby Stonington who were out to discover new islands for the sealing business. One of her owners, and possible builder, was William A. Fanning, a sea captain and shipbuilder who was the son of the noted Pacific explorer Edmund Fanning. William Fanning was also well acquainted with the Palmer family of Stonington, especially Nathaniel Palmer, and would eventually marry Palmer's sister. The small vessel was to be part of an expedition to the bottom of the world, after a previous voyage by the brig *Herselia* had met with great success. The second mate of the *Herselia* was nineteen-year old Nathaniel Palmer, who performed so capably that he was subsequently given command of the *Hero*. Indeed, Palmer is the real "hero" in this story, for his subsequent voyage and explorations in her were just the beginning of an outstanding career that few mariners would ever achieve.

The *Hero* was part of a seven-vessel fleet that included the *Herselia* and three other brigs and two schooners; *Hero* was the smallest of them all. This fleet departed Stonington in August 1820, and though all of them sailed together, each was expected to make its first destination, the Falkland Islands, on its own. The tiny *Hero* more than held her own. From there, the fleet journeyed to the South Shetland Islands and President's Harbor (now New Plymouth), which was to be the base for the American sealing fleet. However, it soon became clear to the fleet's commander, Commodore Benjamin Pendleton, that not enough seals would be found there to fill the holds of all his ships. He then ordered Palmer and the *Hero* to search for other harbors, as the sloop was perfect for maneuvering along the shore of the many small islands in the region. During his explorations, Palmer sighted and entered the fine harbor on what is now Deception Island, one of the South Shetland Islands, the first to visit and explore the island. Yankee Harbor, as it came to be called, is one of the safest harbors in Antarctica, and five of the Stonington fleet would sail here as a base for sealing operations. Following this, the job of *Hero*'s crew was not to catch seals but rather to carry the sealskins that had been gathered at President's Harbor and transport them back to the larger part of the fleet at Deception Island. The full details of these voyages and Captain Palmer's subsequent discoveries are well told by historian John Spears in his biography of Palmer, but the main achievement of Palmer was his discovery of the Antarctic continent, part of which is known to this day as Palmer Land.

With the seal population at President's Harbor soon depleted, it was clear that more seals needed to be found, so Palmer and the *Hero* were sent off yet again on an exploring expedition. It is worthy of mention that, despite her handiness, the sloop was a small vessel indeed, sailing off alone into unknown waters where who knew what hazards—ice, snow, storms, uncharted shoals—might exist. Palmer was undaunted, determined to do his job and find more islands where seals might be found. Pendleton and Palmer agreed, upon surveying the ocean to the south after climbing to the highest point on Deception Island, that there might be suitable islands there, but nothing was certain, and this was an area where no man had seemingly sailed before. *Hero* departed the island in January 1821, and Palmer soon found himself in "extensive mountainous country, more sterile and dismal, if possible, and more heavily loaded with ice and snow than the South Shetlands." He would subsequently sail along the Antarctic Peninsula, transiting the Bransfield and Gerlache straits and entering a bay that offered a sheltered anchorage. During his voyaging, the *Hero* entered a thick fog and was forced to hove to for fear of going ashore. While stuck in the fog, the crew heard bells rung in the distance in response to the ship's bell that was rung to note the hour, as was maritime custom. The sailors thought it eerie—either an echo or perhaps even due to supernatural causes. Later on, human voices were also heard in the distance, to the bewilderment of all. However, when the fog cleared, the mystery was solved, for at anchor just a short distance away were two sizeable Russian navy vessels, the 985-ton warship *Vostok* and the 530-ton supply ship *Mirny*. These were the ships of the First Russian Antarctic Expedition, commanded by Captain Fabian von Bellingshausen under authority of Emperor Alexander I, which circumnavigated Antarctica in 1820–21. While the young captain of the *Hero* was unflappable, the Russians were astounded to find this small American vessel in the region and soon invited her captain to come aboard.

After a friendly meeting, with Bellingshausen requesting to see *Hero*'s logbook that charted the course of her voyage, the Russians conceded to Palmer his astounding feat, though somewhat glum at having been beaten to the punch. Bellingshausen was as gracious as could be, telling Palmer, "What do I see and what do I hear from a boy in his teens? That he is commander of a tiny boat of the size of the launch of my frigate, in which he pushed his way to the pole through storm and ice; has sought and found the point I, in command of one of the best appointed fleets at the disposal of my august master, have for three long, weary years searched day and night for….What shall I say to my master? What will he think of me?

Captain Nathaniel Palmer of Stonington, Connecticut, commander of the sloop *Hero* in his youth and later clipper captain. *From Spears's* Captain Nathaniel Brown Palmer, *1922.*

Be that as it may, my grief is your joy. Wear your laurels with my sincere prayers for your welfare. I name the land you have discovered in honor of yourself, noble boy, Palmer land."

And so the Antarctic Peninsula to this day is named Palmer Land. While modern historians have given credit to Bellingshausen for discovering the Antarctic, having sailed around the continent, it was Palmer who entered its bays, the small *Hero* maneuverable enough to do so. In fact, as is often the case in such discoveries, there is a lot of hair-splitting going on when, really, there is credit enough for all involved. For Bellingshausen, all is not lost, for he twice circumnavigated Antarctica and, in addition to having a fine naval career, is still remembered to this day as an important explorer. As for the *Hero* and Palmer, they returned to Stonington in 1822, after which Palmer took her on a merchant voyage to South America later that year before gaining a larger command. What became of the sloop *Hero* is unclear, but Captain Nathaniel Palmer would continue his stellar career, voyaging again to the South Shetlands and later becoming a notable packet captain, first on the New York to New Orleans run and then with the Dramatic Line running from New York to Liverpool, making a record run in 1840 while in command of the *Siddons*. From there, Palmer went on to command one of the earliest clipper ships, the pioneer *Houqua*, which he designed himself. But he never wrote anything about his exploring voyages in Antarctica. No matter, he and his ship were, indeed, heroes of a sort that brought great credit not just to the men of Stonington but to all seafaring New Englanders and the ships they built, big and small.

Chapter 6

CLIPPER SHIPS, 1850–1920

*T*he evolution of the famed clipper ship class of sailing vessels was one that had many influences over the years, from the late 1700s up until their final development in the 1850s. The clipper ships, by far, have been the most written about, documented and romanticized of any type of American ship since the founding of our country. This is understandable, as their form alone represented many exciting qualities all wrapped up in one package—speed, power and beauty. Add to that their far-flung adventures, notable captains and builders and intimate involvement with the expansion of our country westward, and you end up with an exciting, albeit fleeting, time in American and world maritime history when clipper ships ruled the waves. However, before we discuss the clippers further, it might be best to define just what a clipper ship was.

To move at a "clip" means to move in a specific direction with great haste or speed, so first and foremost, a clipper ship had to be a fast vessel, one whose speed well exceeds that of other vessels of similar size and rig type. Even today, many maritime historians disagree on the designations of which ship might be deemed worthy of the name *clipper*. In the end, the best definition of a clipper, as I've written in my previous book on the subject, is a ship that was designed to sail quickly to her destination without regard to carrying capacity or cost when it came to her building. Clippers were distinguished by their sharp hull forms, which enabled them to sail quickly even if it reduced their cargo capacity, and lofty sail plans, which carried up to sixteen thousand yards of canvas and included a towering mainmast that carried up to six levels of sails, including the aptly named skysails and moonraker sails in some cases. Because these ships were owned by the wealthiest merchants of the day, they were also expensively outfitted and known for their fine figureheads, as well as lavishly outfitted passenger quarters. Finally, the clipper ships were also distinguished by their romantic and glamorous names, which epitomized the movement westward and the national glory and speed aspects that were behind their very existence. This resulted in such delightfully expressive names as *Westward Ho*, *Sovereign of the Seas*, *Flying Dragon*, *Golden Light*, *Golden Fleece*, *Meteor*, *Star of Empire*, *Winged Racer* and *Eagle Wing*. With but few exceptions, these qualities distinguished most of the clipper ships that were built in the 1850s.

While faster sailing ships gradually evolved over the years, it was America's feverish move westward beginning in 1848 with the California Gold Rush that really changed American shipbuilding. While nearly every and any seagoing ship was chartered to carry ordinary citizens turned gold prospectors by 1849 (thus the term "'49ers"), it was also soon realized that cargo ships would be required to carry the supplies that would be needed to build cities overnight. Prior to the gold rush, San Francisco was a sleepy port that was visited by several ships a month. Now, hundreds of ships were arriving a month, and the city—indeed, the soon-to-be state of California—grew by leaps and bounds. It would be East Coast merchants whose products made that growth possible, as the California territory was devoid of any large-scale business or industry. Though there were several routes to get to California—the overland route, the sea and land route across the isthmus of Panama—the preferred way for cargo was the long sea route from America's East Coast, primarily New York or Boston but also Philadelphia and Baltimore, around Cape Horn and up the Pacific to San Francisco. A regular trading vessel might require six months or more to make this arduous sea journey, but the clipper ships cut this time down to as little as three months in rare cases, with four months being about the average. To get such commodities as lumber, liquor, cast-iron stoves, farming and building implements and mining supplies to California, merchants needed fast ships. Once news about the gold rush made it back east, the clipper ships, built in large numbers beginning in 1850, fit the bill. Because demand was so high, so were the freight rates that shipping companies could demand for the use of their fast ships. In turn, the clippers were built for speed, but carrying capacity was less of a concern, as many clippers paid their building costs on their first run out to California. Once the cargo was unloaded at San Francisco, a clipper might travel empty to China, from there bringing

Scene of shipbuilding in East Boston in the 1850s from *Gleason's Pictorial Magazine*. *Author's collection.*

Chinese imports either back to East Coast U.S. ports or even tea to Great Britain. Other clippers headed off to India for goods, while some clippers returned directly to the East Coast, perhaps carrying some passengers or specie but not much in the way of cargo.

Of course, the clipper ship boon would not last forever, and by 1854, most fast ships built were of the medium clipper type. They were still lavishly outfitted but built with an eye toward both speed *and* cargo capacity, with the realization that these ships would eventually be employed in more conventional times when lower freight rates meant that a sharply built ship like an out-and-out clipper with a small cargo hold would not be profitable. The clipper ship era came to an end with the financial Panic of 1857, and in the five years leading up to the Civil War, their fortunes quickly declined. With financial and political skies darkening, many of these once-glorious ships, some driven to excess and now well worn, were relegated to less glamorous duties or sold off to foreign owners. It would not be until after the Civil War that the American merchant fleet would rise again.

SURPRISE

This 1,261-ton clipper was built by Samuel Hall of East Boston in 1850. She has the distinction of being the first true New England clipper ship to make the voyage from the East Coast to San Francisco, as the earlier California clipper ships were New York–built ships. The beautifully finished *Surprise*, which featured a gilded-eagle figurehead and a mainmast seventy-eight feet tall, was owned by the prominent A.A. Low & Brothers merchants of New York. On her maiden voyage to California beginning in December 1850, she arrived in the then record time of ninety-six days and fifteen hours, besting the previous ninety-seven-day record set by the New York clipper *Sea Witch*. From San Francisco, Captain Philip Dumaresq, who supervised the building of the ship, guided his ship to Hong Kong and from thence to London. On this one round-trip voyage, the *Surprise* earned her owners a $50,000 profit above and beyond her building cost and expenses. This clipper, which was originally built for the China trade, had a long-lived career and would make many other voyages before being rebuilt in 1867. On her final voyage in 1875, the old clipper loaded over ten thousand cases of kerosene for Yokohama, Japan, and subsequently wrecked off the harbor there due to an intoxicated pilot. The *Surprise* is also notable as being one of the first clippers

The East Boston–built clipper *Surprise* arriving in England in 1851 after her maiden voyage. *From Morison's* Maritime History of Massachusetts, *1921.*

77

designed by naval architect Samuel Hartt Pook, who would go on to design a number of other famed clippers, including several mentioned below and, later on, navy ships.

NORTHERN LIGHT

Yet another record-breaker designed by Samuel Pook, this beautiful clipper was built in 1851 by the notable firm of E. and H.O. Briggs of South Boston, two brothers who learned their trade on the North River in Scituate. This 1,021-ton clipper was the first of twenty they would build and the most notable for her speed. *Northern Light*'s first run out to California was spoiled by bad weather and the damage she suffered as a result, but her second voyage out was achieved in a very good time of one hundred days. However, it was the homeward voyage from San Francisco to Boston in 1852 that gained *Northern Light*—whose figurehead was a full-length angel bearing a flaming torch held high in one hand—undying fame. On this epic voyage, the clipper made the trip in an incredible seventy-six days and six hours, driven hard by Captain Freeman Hatch in an effort to best her rival, the New York clipper ship *Contest*. When Captain Hatch reported to owner

The record-setting clipper *Northern Light*, built at South Boston in 1851. *From Howe and Matthews's* American Clipper Ships, *1927 (1986).*

Captain James Huckins that he had strained the *Northern Light* on the record voyage, the owner didn't "care a damn" because his rival had been beaten soundly. While the ship may have been weakened in structure, she made another voyage before being sold by Huckins at the incredible price of $60,000. She was subsequently put in the Far East trade, where she made another record run from Boston to Manila under her new owner, Captain Seth Doane. Sadly, this fine ship was lost in 1862 when departing France for New York, sinking after a nighttime collision. As for Captain Hatch, his old command went with him to his grave, in a manner of speaking, in 1889, for on his headstone in Eastham, Massachusetts, the voyage of the *Northern Light* is documented, the epitaph ending with the words "an achievement won by no mortal before or since."

NIGHTINGALE

This fine ship, built by Samuel Hanscom Jr. in the Portsmouth, New Hampshire Customs District, was one clipper that was not intended for the California trade. Instead, *Nightingale* was intended as a passenger vessel, built as a showpiece and a transatlantic packet for the 1851 World's Fair in London, famed for its Crystal Palace exhibition. As a result, this 1,060-ton yacht-like clipper, named after the famed singer Jenny Lind, known as the "Swedish Nightingale," was lavishly outfitted with the finest woods and most modern passenger cabins found in a sailing ship. In fact, her costs were so high that delays resulted, and she ended up missing out on the World's Fair altogether due to the resulting financial mess. In terms of her building without regard to cost, *Nightingale* epitomized this aspect of the clipper ship era, she being a beautiful and sharply built ship, featuring a bust of Jenny Lind as her figurehead, while the stern had a carving of the singer in a reclining pose with a nightingale perched on her finger and the name of the ship carved in blue and gold letters. Subsequently put in the China trade, *Nightingale* made a name as a fast ship even if she set no records. This famed clipper also had a long life. Just before the Civil War, she was sold off due to her high operating cost and low cargo-carrying capacity. She was subsequently operated by a New York owner as a slave ship, no doubt due to her speed, for a year before being captured by the U.S. Navy off the African coast in 1861 with a cargo of 961 human beings (with 801 survivors eventually landed at Monrovia). Now legally condemned and subsequently owned by the navy, *Nightingale* operated as a naval vessel during the Civil

Currier & Ives lithograph of the beautiful 1851-built New Hampshire clipper *Nightingale*. *Author's collection.*

War, being sold afterward to private parties and returning to the merchant trade in 1865 before being sold to Norwegian owners in 1876. With her rig cut down to that of a bark and her figurehead removed (today it is in a private collection), the old clipper was still a useful ship and continued her career longer than most clippers, working in the North Atlantic lumber trade before being abandoned at sea in 1893 after a forty-two-year career. It is fairly safe to say that no clipper had such a varied, both famous and infamous, career as that of the *Nightingale*, and it is no wonder that she, too, was the subject of a popular Currier & Ives print.

FLYING CLOUD

The most famous American clipper ship of all time, and undoubtedly one of the most famous ships in the world, the *Flying Cloud* was the product of famed clipper builder Donald McKay of East Boston. The 1,782-ton extreme clipper, adorned with the figurehead of an angel blowing a trumpet, was originally built for Boston merchant Enoch Train in 1851, but even before the *Flying Cloud* was finished, the New York firm of Grinnell, Minturn & Co.

offered Train $90,000 for the ship. It was an offer Train couldn't pass up, yet one that he would soon come to regret. This beautiful clipper had a rakish appearance with a mainmast eighty-eight feet tall and was commanded by Marblehead, Massachusetts native Captain Josiah Creesy, a noted driver in the China trade. The very first voyage of the *Flying Cloud* was a historic one, as she made the journey from New York to San Francisco in eighty-nine days and twenty-one hours, shattering the previous record. Incredibly, on the clipper's fourth California run in 1854, she did even better, arriving in eighty-nine days and eight hours. So famous was the *Flying Cloud* that California merchants advertised their goods as arriving on that clipper to hype sales. With these two passages, the *Flying Cloud* established herself as the fastest clipper of all time and to this day is the posterchild for the clipper ship era, deservedly so, even if her record was bested by several hours (see "*Andrew Jackson*"). The *Flying Cloud* would continue in the California and Far East trade for a number of years and made some other record runs along the way, but with the onset of the financial Panic of 1857, she was left idle in New York for over two years. Afterward, she was sold to British owners and put into the Australia trade. The *Flying Cloud* at the end of her career was put in the North Atlantic timber trade between Canada and England, with

Currier & Ives lithograph view of the famed clipper *Flying Cloud*, built in 1851. She was sold for $90,000 while still on the builder's ways. *Courtesy Library of Congress.*

the end coming in 1874 when she went ashore off New Brunswick during a severe storm and was subsequently condemned and burned for her metal fittings in 1875.

Great Republic

This clipper ship, built by Donald McKay in East Boston in 1853, lived up to the name "Great" in *Great Republic* in every way. Coming in at a whopping 4,555 tons, not only was she the biggest clipper built, but at the time of her building she was also the largest wooden ship in the world. She was named after the Great Republic of the United States, and some other measurements and features speak to her size, including a 131-foot-tall mainmast, a spread of nearly 16,000 yards of sailcloth, some 1.5 million feet of pine lumber going into her construction, over 300 tons of iron fittings, four anchors and even a small engine to hoist her sails and help load cargo. Even with that, the ship, the first and only clipper to have four masts (technically a four-masted bark) instead of the normal three, required a crew of 130 men and boys; a normal clipper carried well under half that amount. Like many other clippers, the *Great Republic* was also lavishly outfitted, having a figurehead consisting of an eagle's head with an open beak just over 5 feet long and a large eagle with extended wings carved on her stern, passenger cabins with mahogany wainscoting and recessed sofas with velvet covers, as well as stained-glass panels and mirrors.

The progress of the building of this behemoth was well reported on by the Boston press, and the day of her launching was made a public holiday, with tens of thousands of people, including builder Donald McKay in his traditional top hat, attending the event. Interestingly, the *Great Republic* was not intended for the California trade but rather for the Australian trade, and she was built on speculation by McKay, the ship captained by his brother Lauchlan McKay. After her launch, the great clipper was towed to New York, where finishing touches were made before she was loaded with a cargo bound for Liverpool, England. The ship was even opened to the public for several days. Visitors paid a small fee, with all the proceeds going to the Seamen's Aid Society in New York.

Sadly, before she could ever sail, a fire broke out ashore near her wharf, with winds carrying blazing cinders onto the deck of the clipper. While men tried to save the ship, her great masts had to be cut away, and she was eventually scuttled, the ship burning to the waterline. Donald McKay took a

View of the clipper *Great Republic* under construction at the yard of McKay from *Gleason's Pictorial*, 1853. *Author's collection.*

The clipper *Great Republic*, rebuilt under the supervision of Nathaniel Palmer after catching fire in New York. *From Spears's* Captain Nathaniel Brown Palmer, *1922.*

huge loss on the ship, over $450,000 on ship and cargo, and what was left of the *Great Republic* went to the insurance company. How this behemoth might have performed can never be known, but like the phoenix bird, this ship, too, rose from the ashes. Purchased by A.A. Low & Brothers of New York as she lay, she was raised and rebuilt under the supervision of Captain Nathaniel Palmer of Antarctic fame. The rebuilt, or second, *Great Republic* was reduced from four decks to three and had her tonnage reduced to 3,356, still the largest American clipper.

Finally, she was able to set sail on her maiden voyage in February 1855, now requiring only a fifty-man crew. The *Great Republic* would have a successful career, carrying huge amounts of cargo and making some good California and Far East passages. In 1869, the *Great Republic* was sold to foreign owners, and her name was changed to *Denmark*. Her career lasted another three years before she began to leak while on a voyage from Rio de Janeiro to St. John's, New Brunswick, and subsequently foundered. While the career of this great clipper is filled with "what if" questions that can never be answered in terms of speed and performance, her sheer size and Donald McKay's daring in building such an unconventional vessel are part of the lore and legend of the clipper ship era. Her original eagle figurehead, saved when the ship was burned, can be seen today at the Mystic Seaport Museum in Connecticut.

ANDREW JACKSON

This clipper was built at Mystic, Connecticut, by Irons & Grinnell in 1855 for New York owners. Classified as a medium clipper, the *Andrew Jackson* measured 1,679 tons and, of course, had a figurehead of the famed general turned president. She was a very well-built ship, but despite her excellent reputation and record-setting feat, she is largely overshadowed by her competitor *Flying Cloud* and other New York clippers built by more famed or notable builders. However, the record of the *Andrew Jackson* cannot be denied. She was employed in the California trade almost entirely during her career under the American flag, making seven round-trip voyages between 1855 and 1862. Her most notable feat came in 1860, when she made the run from New York to San Francisco in eighty-nine days and four hours under the command of the hard-driving Captain John Williams, thereby setting the all-time record by beating the *Flying Cloud*'s best run by four hours. While this record run was haggled over among historians and maritime enthusiasts

Drawing by William A. Coulter of the Connecticut clipper *Andrew Jackson* arriving in San Francisco. From the *San Francisco Call*, March 13, 1897. *Courtesy Library of Congress.*

The Famous Old Clipper Andrew Jackson Making Port in October, 1867. The Pilot-Boat Caleb Curtis Is Putting a Pilot Aboard. The Fannie Is in the Distance. The Drawing Is From a Picture Found Among His Brother's Effects a Couple of Days Ago by Sam Wheeland of Collins & Wheeland.

from New York and Boston for decades after, documentary evidence would eventually surface that indeed proved that the *Flying Cloud* had been beaten.

This feat alone makes the *Andrew Jackson* a worthy addition to this list, but there is more to her accomplishments than this one record run. The clipper was in fact a very consistent performer on the California route, averaging about 105 days on all her voyages, a number very close to that of the *Flying Cloud* and other notable clippers. Was the *Andrew Jackson* the fastest clipper ever? As I've documented in my book, the *Flying Cloud*, which made two California passages in 89 days, and several other Donald McKay–built clippers were certainly faster vessels overall, but the fine performance of this Connecticut clipper puts her in their elite company. In 1863, like so many other American ships during the Civil War, the *Andrew Jackson* was sold to British owners and was subsequently lost in 1868 after going ashore while bound from Shanghai to Glasgow.

Chapter 7

NAVAL SHIPS OF THE CIVIL WAR, 1861–1865

Though overshadowed by the famed and bloody land battles, the Civil War at sea was also a critical component in the Union strategy to defeat the South. While the Confederate states had virtually no navy and few merchant ships at the outset of the war, the Union navy was also small, having fewer than one hundred ships overall, with just under half of them warships fit for action. However, the industrial might of the Northern states meant that they could in short order build more ships, which they did, adding the *Unadilla*-class "ninety-day" gunboats and *City*-class ironclad gunboats to the fleet in quick time. However, the Confederacy was forced to build its warships, mostly steam-powered wooden vessels, overseas. The Union plan for its navy was simple; the aptly named Anaconda Plan was designed to forcefully squeeze the Southern states into submission by cutting off their overseas trade. To that end, Union warships were employed as blockade ships, their fleets sent to such Southern ports as Charleston, Wilmington, Mobile and New Orleans to stop Confederate merchant ships from leaving and to prevent merchant ships from bringing goods into port. While the blockade efforts were technically a failure, as most ships that did try running the blockade were successful, the overall objective was achieved, as many ships did not even try to run the blockade, fearful of the results, and the Southern economy suffered greatly for it. Smaller Union warships, including ironclad gunboats, were also employed in countless locales from Virginia and the Carolinas to the Gulf Coast area in river warfare, with major operations on the Mississippi River designed to cut the Confederacy in half. Some of the greatest naval actions of the war took place with the capture of such key cities as New Orleans and Mobile, Alabama. Of course, naval ships were also employed in support of Union troop landings, providing bombardment support for the Union army at such places as Vicksburg, Fort Fisher and Charleston.

On the Confederate side, their main goal was to put a hurt on the merchant fleet of the Northern states, and this they did quite successfully. Confederate raiders, powerful steam-powered warships, were built in Britain, and though they would never enter a Southern port, the raids they made on Northern shipping, though not enough to turn the tide of war, were significant. Because of these raiders, the American merchant fleet declined by nearly 50 percent, partly due to the depredations themselves but also because of the resulting high insurance rates, which caused many American ships to be sold to foreign owners. The Civil War was also a turning point in shipbuilding, marking the change from the wooden navy to the modern iron and, later, steel navy, but also spelled the end, once and for all, of the sailing navy. The last naval warship built that was sail-powered was the corvette *Constellation* (now a museum ship in Baltimore) in 1854, and by the time of the Civil War, the primary warship was the steam-screw sloop-of-war. Such wooden warships, like the *Hartford*, had three masts and looked like sailing ships but had a large funnel amidships, indicative of the powerful steam engine that was their main form of propulsion. This type of warship had the advantage of being maneuverable whether there was a wind or not, unlike the old ships in the sailing navy.

However, it was during the Civil War that the idea of an armored warship would be put to the test, with the result that wooden warships would soon be a thing of the past. The actions of the Confederate ironclad CSS *Virginia* and the devastation it wrought on the Union fleet at Norfolk, Virginia, followed by the duel between the *Virginia* and the Union ironclad *Monitor* in March 1862 would change naval history forever. With the eventual shift to ironclad warships, New England shipyards were not at first in the forefront of this new technology, but nevertheless some of the products from its shipyards played a key role during the war at sea from 1861 to 1865.

MERRIMACK (LATER CSS VIRGINIA)

This steam screw frigate led an interesting, if short-lived, two-part life and in each of them was a revolutionary warship. The *Merrimack* was built at the Boston Navy Yard in 1855 and was the first U.S. Navy frigate to be powered by screw propellers; earlier steam frigates had side-wheel paddles. Coming in at 3,200 tons and 275 feet long, the *Merrimack* was the first of six such ships built for the navy and was also notable for being the first navy ship armed with modern guns that were solely shell-firing. She first served in the Pacific Squadron before the Civil War but was laid up for repairs after returning from there to the Norfolk Navy Yard in Virginia in 1860. When the Civil War broke out, she was blockaded in Norfolk, unable to depart earlier due to her engines being in bad shape. As Confederate troops from Virginia sought to capture the navy yard, the *Merrimack* was deliberately set afire and burned to the waterline as Union sailors retreated in April 1861. Thus ended the first life of the *Merrimack*.

However, once the navy yard was in Confederate hands, they were desperate for warships of any kind and came up with a plan to convert the hull of the *Merrimack* into an ironclad ram. Desperately short of manufactured iron, the fledgling Confederate navy had to resort to collecting scrap metal to get enough iron to rebuild the ship. Since the *Merrimack*'s hull below water was intact, the Confederates designed a casemate type of ironclad, distinguished by its armored gundeck, built right over the hull of the sunken ship, with slanted sides and slits for fourteen large guns, some of which were from the original armament of the *Merrimack*. Most interesting was the iron ram installed on the prow of the vessel, a feature that dated back several thousand years to the triremes of the ancient Greek and Phoenician navies.

Finally, in February 1862, the rebuilt *Merrimack* was commissioned in the Confederate navy as the *Virginia*. From this point forward, some may be confused by the ship's name change, but the explanation is simple; while the Confederates used the new name, the Northern press would still refer to the ironclad by her original name of *Merrimack*. The *Virginia*'s first operational sortie took place on March 8–9, 1862, during the historic naval Battle of Hampton Roads. On the first day of the battle, the *Virginia* sailed into Hampton Roads as the flagship of a six-ship flotilla and made history by destroying the Union navy wooden warships *Cumberland* and *Congress* and damaging the *Minnesota*. The *Virginia* was also damaged during this first action, and her commanding officer was wounded. Subsequently withdrawing for the night, the *Virginia* hoped to finish off the Union fleet the next day. However, it was not to be as the Union ironclad *Monitor* arrived that night from the Brooklyn Navy Yard, her crew able to see a sky lit up with the flames from the still-burning Union warships.

The following day, March 9, 1862, was a historic one that would see the first ever battle between two ironclad ships. The two ships fought at close quarters

A lithograph of the steam frigate *Merrimack* as she appeared before the Civil War. *Courtesy Naval History and Heritage Command archives.*

The battle between the Confederate ironclad *Virginia* (ex. *Merrimack*) at left and the Union ironclad *Monitor*. *Courtesy Naval History and Heritage Command archives.*

for hours; the *Monitor*, often described as a "cheese-box" or "tin can on a raft," sat low to the water and had a single round turret armed with two cannons. Its low profile and ability to maneuver made it a difficult target for the *Virginia* to sink, while the slower *Virginia*'s heavy casemate armor protected the ship from numerous hits by the *Monitor*'s guns. The engagement, one of the most famous of the war, ended in a draw when the *Monitor* withdrew after her captain was wounded by a gunpowder explosion. The *Virginia*'s captain had hoped to continue the fight, but fearful of grounding his heavy ship on a sandbar at low tide, he returned to Norfolk and the Union blockade remained, battered but intact. The *Virginia* in the next several months would try to break the blockade, at one point even taunting the Union navy, but was unsuccessful. In May 1862, with Union troops advancing on Norfolk, the *Virginia* was destroyed by the Confederates to prevent her from falling into Union hands. Remnants of the ironclad, including an anchor, survive to this day.

HARTFORD

This 2,900-ton, steam-powered sloop-of-war was built at the Boston Navy Yard in 1858–59 and was stationed in the Far East when the Civil War broke out. Recalled home, she arrived at Philadelphia in December 1861 and, after being outfitted for wartime service, was sent to the West Gulf Blockading Squadron as the flagship for Flag Officer David Farragut, who had previously served aboard the frigate *Essex* during the War of 1812 as a young boy. The primary goal of this squadron was the capture of New Orleans, which would be accomplished in April 1862. With the fleet assembled at the mouth of the Mississippi River, their first task was to get past the Confederate forts of St. Philip and Jackson. During these operations, Farragut and the *Hartford* were in the thick of things, fending off an attack by the Confederate ironclad *Manassas* and running aground near Fort St. Philip and narrowly being set on fire. Having run this gauntlet, the next day *Hartford* and the other ships of the Union fleet knocked out the Confederate land-based artillery batteries, and the city of New Orleans fell to Union forces, a great blow to the Confederacy. Following this, Farragut and the *Hartford* took part in the operations around Vicksburg beginning in June 1862, and the *Hartford* was the only ship to run the gauntlet of Confederate artillery. The patrols *Hartford* ran between Port Hudson and Vicksburg denied essential supplies to the beleaguered city, which finally surrendered on July 4, 1863.

With two major objectives of the Union Anaconda Plan now achieved, Farragut and *Hartford* now had as their next objective the important Confederate city of Mobile, Alabama. In this decisive action, the wooden *Hartford* led a flotilla of eighteen ships, including four ironclads, in August 1864 against a Confederate force led by the new ironclad *Tennessee* and several gunboats, all backed by Confederate artillery in Fort Gaines and Fort Morgan at the mouth of Mobile Bay. The heated battle lasted three hours, the Union navy suffering over three hundred casualties, many from the sunken monitor *Tecumseh*. The *Hartford* played a large part in the battle, which resulted in one fort and the *Tennessee* being captured, with twelve crewmen subsequently awarded the Medal of Honor. Among them were Pilot Martin Freeman, a civilian who from the maintop of *Hartford* guided the flagship and the fleet into Mobile Bay under heavy fire, as well as an African American sailor, Landsman John Lawson, who, though severely wounded in the leg while serving as an ammunition handler, stayed at his post and continued to help supply the guns of the flagship. However, it was David Farragut who would help immortalize *Hartford*. Lashed to the ship's mast during the battle after having climbed into the rigging (to the horror of the ship's officers!) to get a better view of the battle, at a crucial point in the fighting he is said to have cried, "Damn the

The steam frigate *Hartford*, flagship of David Farragut in the Civil War. *Courtesy Naval History and Heritage Command archives.*

torpedoes, full speed ahead!" This battle cry afterward became legendary in naval history. While his exact words have been debated for over one hundred years by naval historians, there is no debating the historical significance of Farragut and *Hartford* as a fighting duo.

Following this battle, the wartime service of the *Hartford* was at an end. She would continue in her naval service for over twenty years before being laid up at Mare Island, California, and subsequently sent to Charleston, South Carolina, as a station ship in 1912. Despite efforts by President Franklin Roosevelt to save the ship and turn her into a museum, after his death these efforts fell by the wayside, and the *Hartford*, then at the Norfolk Navy Yard, slowly fell to pieces and sank at her berth in 1956.

KEARSARGE

A *Mohican*-class sloop-of-war, the 1,550-ton *Kearsarge* was built at the Portsmouth Naval Shipyard in New Hampshire in 1861, one of many ships built under the emergency shipbuilding program enacted at the beginning of the war by the U.S. Navy. Commissioned and ready for service in January 1862, the ship carried a main armament consisting of two eleven-inch Dahlgren guns and was sent to European waters to search for and destroy Confederate commerce raiders. Her first assignment sent her to the coast of Spain and Gibraltar, helping to blockade the raider *Sumter*. When that raider was abandoned there by the Confederates in December 1862, her commander, Captain Raphael Semmes, made his way to England to his new command, the raider *Alabama*. While that raider would make a name for herself over the next year, *Kearsarge* remained on the northern European coast, and when the *Alabama* put into Cherbourg, France, for repairs, *Kearsarge*, now commanded by Captain John Winslow, was just outside French territorial waters waiting for her to come out to sea. In preparation for the Battle of Cherbourg that was soon to come, while in port at the Azores, Captain Winslow wisely gave his ship extra armored protection in the form of several tiers of chain cable amidships to protect her engine machinery, hidden by wooden boards painted the same color as the hull of the ship. Finally, on June 19, 1864, Semmes conned *Alabama* out of Cherbourg and immediately went on the attack, firing on *Kearsarge* while the two ships were sailing on opposite courses. The *Kearsarge* held her fire until she got closer, with the two ships subsequently maneuvering in circles, each trying to cross the other's bow to

Popular print of antagonists at the Battle of Cherbourg in 1864, with *Kearsarge* at left and a sinking *Alabama*. *Courtesy Naval History and Heritage Command archives.*

give a raking fire. *Alabama*'s gunnery was poor; her gunpowder and shells had deteriorated in condition, having been too long in storage at sea. Though *Alabama*'s shells hit the *Kearsarge*, its armor did its job, and the cannonballs failed to do major damage. Meanwhile, the fire of the *Kearsarge* after an hour of battle reduced the *Alabama* to a sinking wreck. Though Captain Semmes surrendered his ship, the *Alabama* soon sank by the stern. While most of the *Alabama*'s crew were rescued by the *Kearsarge*, Semmes and forty-one of his men were rescued by a nearby British yacht that had witnessed the action and carried them safely to England. During this battle, seventeen *Kearsarge* crewmen earned the Medal of Honor, including captain of gun #1 Robert Strahan, sponger James Lee and gun-loader Joachim Pease, a Black sailor from Cape Verde who had a "reputation as one of the best men in the ship," according to his medal citation.

After this epic battle, the *Kearsarge* stayed on the French coast searching for the raider *Florida* before eventually returning to Boston for repairs. The sloop-of-war would serve the navy until being wrecked off the Nicaraguan coast in 1894. The famed killer of the *Alabama* is well remembered to this day in New Hampshire, with the state's Mount Kearsarge named in her honor.

Chapter 8

THE LAST DAYS OF THE
SQUARE-RIGGERS, 1865–1894

*F*ollowing the end of the Civil War, the American merchant fleet was in shambles, its former glory all but vanished. According to historian William Fairburn, the American merchant fleet at the dawn of the clipper ship era carried over 92 percent of the country's imports and exports combined, but by the start of the Civil War, that had been reduced to 66 percent. Much of the prewar reduction may be attributed to the hard times after the financial Panic of 1857, which led to many U.S. ships, mostly square-riggers, being sold to foreign owners. By 1865, American ships carried only 27 percent of our nation's commerce.

After the war, attempts to rebuild the merchant fleet were made, but it was soon clear that the day of the sailing ship was coming to an end, and the first of these ships to go would be the glorious square-rigged ships, which required bigger crews and were more costly in operation and upkeep than their schooner cousins. One of the major factors in the decline of these ships was the rise of new transportation technology in the form of the steamship and the railroad. More paddlewheel (and later propeller-powered) steamships were being built in this country after 1870 than sailing ships, and this was true in most New England states as well, with the exception of Maine. However, the square-riggers would hold their own for another twenty years or so because of the emergence of an improved model known as the "Down Easter." Some of the ships that were built during this post–Civil War time were holdovers from the prior decade and might be called "half clippers," but most were of the new type, these ships having the good cargo-carrying capacity that was required in those times yet also having good lines and the ability to sail well and reach their intended destination in good time. Another change in these ships were their naming practices. Unlike the high-flown names of the clipper ships, these ships mostly had more practical and workaday names, often named after their principal owners.

With these changes, the Down Easters were fast ships that were economical to build, more so than the iron ships built in Britain with which they were in competition, and some of them made fast passages that were close to that of the clippers of the 1850s. As to cargoes, these ships were the bulk carriers of the day, operating in a variety of trades. The California grain trade to Europe was by far the most important but also the case oil (kerosene in tins) trade to the Far East, lumber in the North Atlantic and Pacific Northwest trades, the coal trade from England and Australia, the Alaska salmon cannery trade, the Peruvian guano trade and all sorts of general cargo, including over one hundred locomotives carried from New York for California and Oregon railroads.

SEMINOLE

Built by Maxon, Fish & Co. at Mystic, Connecticut, in 1865, this 1,439-ton ship was one of the finest ever built in Connecticut. Though her appearance was that of a clipper, *Seminole* was actually a very good cargo ship, as was typical of Down Easters, able to carry a load of over 2,000 tons deadweight. Built for New York owners, the ship featured an Indian warrior as a figurehead and cost $125,000 to build. Specially built for the California trade, the *Seminole* made twenty-one voyages between New York and San Francisco from 1865 to 1887 and made a mark for fast passages on her maiden run, arriving in San Francisco in ninety-eight days in March 1866. On that voyage—one of only two that were made to California in under one hundred days by sailing ships in the post–Civil War era—the *Seminole* carried as part of her cargo locomotive #10 for the Central Pacific Railroad, weighing some 35 tons. On several of her voyages, she went from San Francisco to England before returning to New York. In 1887, the *Seminole* was sold to Pacific coast interests and home-ported out of San Francisco. However, the old ship, subsequently cut down to a bark rig, had some life in her yet, carrying coal between Puget Sound and San Francisco, as well as carrying lumber to South America and Australia. She was sold twice again, in 1898 and 1899, with her final voyage in North American waters being

The Down Easter *Seminole*, built at Mystic, Connecticut, in 1865. *From Matthews's* American Merchant Ships, *1931 (1987).*

from Vancouver to Australia with a load of lumber. On her final voyage, *Seminole* was towed from Newcastle to Adelaide, Australia, where she was turned into a store-ship, her sailing days over.

GREAT ADMIRAL

One of the last great ships to be built in the Boston area, this handsome 1,497-ton vessel was built by noted clipper ship builder Robert Jackson of East Boston for William F. Weld & Co. in 1869. The *Great Admiral* was really a medium clipper rather than a true Down Easter and had a mainmast ninety feet tall that carried a skysail, with the ship overall carrying close to eight thousand yards of canvas. Considered the finest American ship afloat at the time of her launching, the *Great Admiral* was nicknamed the "Weld yacht," so finely fitted out was she, and was originally intended to be named the *Jason*, to go along with another ship of the Weld fleet, the *Golden Fleece*. However, with the fame of the naval hero of the Civil War David Farragut, who was nicknamed the "Great Admiral," the ship's name was changed, and the ship

One of Boston's last great ships, the Weld-owned *Great Admiral*, built in 1869. *From Matthews's* American Merchant Ships, *1931 (1987)*.

carried a life-sized carving of him as a figurehead. The *Great Admiral* flew the Black Horse flag of the Weld fleet from her inception until her sale in 1897 and over those years made eighty-two voyages, many to San Francisco and the Far East but also many others to Europe and Australia, traveling some 727,000 miles. Though not a record-maker, the ship made good passages, suffered no major incidents and paid her building cost many times over. Sold for a mere $12,500 to Captain E.R. Sterling in 1897, the *Great Admiral* was put in the Pacific Northwest coal and lumber trade. She met her end in 1906 on a voyage from Port Townsend to San Pedro, California, when she foundered in heavy seas while carrying a cargo of lumber, with the loss of two of her crew.

GLORY OF THE SEAS

This ship was the last to be built by Donald McKay of East Boston. Launched in 1869, she came in at 2,002 tons and carried some eight thousand yards of canvas. There is some debate among historians about her hull model. Frederick Matthews, in his account of *Glory of the Seas*, states that "she was in fact of full model and on Cape Horn voyages generally loaded 3000 tons in deadweight cargo....Her later cargoes ran between 3300 and 3600 tons." This amount of cargo certainly fit in with the ideal of the typical Down Easter, but the ship really was an evolved clipper. As Michael Jay Mjelde documents in his book, "McKay came to imagine *Glory of the Seas* as a prototype of a large grain carrier, bigger than any vessel then sailing in the California grain fleet....McKay was convinced that this *Glory of the Seas*... could be the acme of medium clipper construction." So, medium clipper this ship was, and a good one too, though she would prove to be uneconomical in later years due to her size and was often laid up for this reason.

The ship was an attractive one in every way, with a graceful elliptical stern and a bow featuring a figurehead of a beautiful female in flowing robes. Like many of McKay's ships, it was named by his wife, Mary. While many historians have questioned, and rightfully so, Donald McKay's business sense, there is no denying the fact that he built ships that made an impression. McKay believed in his creation so much that he built the *Glory* on speculation, with no intended buyer in mind, yet hopeful her performance would bring one soon enough. It was a big gamble that would not pay off, as McKay was already insolvent and his two previous ships had been severe disappointments in terms of speed. The *Glory of the Seas* would turn out be a solid performer, and though she does hold the record for a voyage from San Francisco to Australia—thirty-five days in 1875—she set no other records during her long career. However, in 1873–74, she did make a ninety-six-day passage from New York to San Francisco, the fastest of any ship in the post–Civil War era and the ninth fastest on record.

The *Glory* was not only employed in the California grain trade, carrying those cargoes from San Francisco to Liverpool or Queenstown, but frequently carried coal from Liverpool or Cardiff, Wales, back to San Francisco. Her most harrowing passage was in 1874, when her cargo of coal nearly combusted. The ship was saved when the coal was doused with water by the crew for several days. Interestingly, on the ship's maiden voyage, Donald McKay journeyed on his new creation to California, officially listed as "Captain," though a sailing master was really in charge. On his return the

A painting of the clipper *Glory of the Seas* taking on a pilot at San Francisco. *From McKay's* Some Famous Sailing Ships, *1928*.

ship was idled, the subject of legal battles over McKay's insolvent finances. It was eventually turned over to a group of investors after he failed to find a buyer at his asking price of $190,000.

Once new ownership was established, Captain Josiah Knowles took command of the *Glory of the Seas* and was aboard during her best years and finest passages. In 1884, the ship was sold and subsequently made her last Cape Horn run under Captain Joshua Freeman before being engaged in the coastal trade until 1902. She made her last voyage as a sailing ship in 1908 and was later converted to a floating salmon cannery before being laid up for good at Endolyne, Washington. She came to an inglorious end in 1923 when she was burned on a local beach for her metal fittings, though her beautiful figurehead had been saved by a private collector and is now housed at the India House, a private club, in New York City.

WITH THE COMPLETION OF the medium clippers or Down Easters listed here, the wooden shipbuilding business was at an end in southern New England. Rhode Island's shipbuilding industry was on the decline well before the

1850s, while Connecticut, which built some important Down Easters but did so for only a few years, built its last square-rigger at Mystic in 1869. Farther north, New Hampshire built its last square-rigger in 1877, this being the white-painted *Paul Jones*. In Massachusetts, old traditions would die hard, and it would not be until 1883 that the last square-rigger, the *Mary L. Cushing*, would slide down the ways at Newburyport. In fact, that maritime center held out longer than Boston, whose final square-rigger, the *Luzon*, was built at East Boston in 1881. Indeed, the closing of shipyards in New England during the 1870s and 1880s offered a sorry spectacle in terms of both job loss and the end of traditions that had been carried on for over two hundred years. Researcher Henry Hall commented on this decline of New England shipbuilding in grim fashion. About New Hampshire shipbuilding, he stated, "There is now almost no ship work done at Portsmouth. The yards are abandoned except in one or two cases....The boat-shops are going to decay." About Boston, he comments that "after 1865 the industry was a struggling one, and steadily declined. High wages and strikes among the carpenters and caulkers gave the finishing blow; nearly all the old builders went out of business so far as new work was concerned, and the few that kept their yards going have had a hard time of it." Of the North River area of Massachusetts, he states, "At Scituate, Cohasset, and Duxbury there is nothing left of the ancient industry....The industry is dead and nothing has been built since 1876." About Mystic, Connecticut, Hall states that "the old ship-yards are deserted, the town has lost nearly all its carpenters and its growth is arrested." Only in Maine, especially in the city of Bath, as is shown below, was the construction of major square-rigged ships carried on in a significant way. That state built some 177 Down Easters, or 80 percent of these ships, from 1870 to 1902 and 100 percent of them from 1885 onward.

A.G. Ropes

This 2,342-ton ship, built in Bath by John McDonald for the shipbuilding and mercantile firm of I.F. Chapman & Co. in 1884, was one of the famed sailing ships of her day. Nearly her entire career was spent in the California grain trade for which she was designed, making many voyages between New York, San Francisco and Great Britain. The only exceptions to this were several voyages carrying case oil to the Far East. According to Frederick Matthews, such a voyage in 1901 to Yokohama, Japan, was particularly harrowing, as Captain David Rivers had no qualified first or second mates and mostly

Postcard view of the big Maine Down Easter *A.G. Ropes*, built at Bath in 1884, off Provincetown, Massachusetts. *Author's collection.*

novices in his foreign crew, and he was on duty for as many as three straight days without a rest. The *A.G. Ropes*, named after a partner in the firm, was one of the fastest ships afloat, her main rival being the *Henry B. Hyde* (see following). She made consistently good passages, averaging 120 days from New York to San Francisco, with two voyages under 108 days. On one fast voyage from San Francisco to Britain, the crew of the *Ropes* rescued the crew of a British bark off Cape Horn. The feat was so dangerous and skillful that Rivers was awarded a gold watch by the British government in appreciation, while four of his crew received medals for the roles they played.

Though her Cape Horn passages were many, the *Ropes* had only one disastrous voyage, that of 204 days in 1899–1900, her last voyage on that route. Her rudder was damaged in heavy seas off the Horn and had to be jury-rigged, she was nearly driven ashore on the Falklands and she was almost crushed by the many ice packs in the region. Admitting defeat, Captain Rivers turned his battered ship around and headed across the Atlantic and rounded the Cape of Good Hope, taking the circular route around the world to finally reach San Francisco. Though the passage was difficult, it was just one of the countless examples that showed both the mettle and resourcefulness of Yankee ship captains, many of them from Maine, and the rugged nature of Maine-built Down Easters.

The *Ropes* met her end as a sailing ship in 1905 when she was badly damaged in a typhoon shortly after departing Hong Kong for Baltimore and was subsequently towed to Kobe, Japan. Captain Rivers patched the

A.G. Ropes up the best he could and nursed her homeward to New York, and after her arrival in 1906, she was deemed not worthy of repair and was sold to the Luckenbach Company and converted into a barge. While under tow in late 1913, the old *A.G. Ropes* was lost off the New Jersey coast along with her three-man crew.

HENRY B. HYDE

Yet another big ship from the yard operated by John McDonald in Bath, the 1884-built *Henry B. Hyde* was the most famous Down Easter ever built. It should not be surprising that McDonald built such a ship, for the Nova Scotian native knew his craft well, having trained with fellow countryman Donald McKay at his East Boston shipyard before moving north. His last work with McKay was on the big *Great Republic* (see previous). The *Henry B. Hyde*, named after a life insurance company president, was of 2,580 tons, 290 feet long, with a hold 29 feet deep. She cost some $125,000 to build and was designed for the California grain trade. She made sixteen runs on the Cape Horn route during her service, most from New York. Her average time to California in all these voyages was 124 days, while her fastest time was 105 days. Though her average times are slower than that of the *A.G. Ropes*, many experts believe that the *Henry B. Hyde* was actually the faster ship. However, it would appear that the differences between the two ships in terms of speed were negligible at best.

Most of the *Hyde*'s captains hailed from Searsport, Maine, with part-owner Captain Phineas Pendleton and his cousin Captain John Pendleton being the most noted. Captain John Pendleton was in command when the *Henry B. Hyde* made her fast passage from San Francisco to New York in eighty-eight days in 1888, carrying over sixty thousand bags of sugar. The ship was also subject to many mishaps and harrowing events during her years of operations, including a three-way collision in San Francisco harbor while being towed in 1886, a fire in her coal cargo in 1900 and a near coal cargo fire while attempting a run around Cape Horn in 1902.

Her final end came in February 1904 while under tow from New York to Baltimore to load another coal cargo. The ship broke adrift during a storm and drove ashore near Cape Henry, Virginia. While the crew were saved, the old Down Easter could not be. Stormy seas washed sand into the beached ship, and subsequent operations, hampered by stormy weather yet again, caused her to break her back. The ship was left where she lay, the wreck later

The famed Down Easter *Henry B. Hyde* in the process of furling sails, her deck nearly awash in heavy seas. *Author's collection.*

dynamited so that her masts and other components could be salvaged. The end of this famed Down Easter was a significant news event of the day and the wreck was well documented, with photographs published in newspapers across the country.

SHENANDOAH

A product of the famed shipyard of Arthur Sewall & Co. at Bath in 1890, this ship was the fourth four-masted bark ever built in the United States, and the largest ship of the day, at least for a short time. The *Shenandoah* measured 3,258 tons and was 300 feet long, with the forward masts towering some 214 feet skyward, including a skysail mast, and the ship carried some 11,000 yards of canvas. Over 800 tons of white oak and other hardwoods were used in her construction, as well as over 1 million feet of pine planking. The ship, which cost $175,000, was the subject of much debate, with many in the shipping community believing she was too big, too long and would not be maneuverable in heavy seas. These fears would prove to be unfounded.

The Sewall-built four-masted bark *Shenandoah*, built at Bath in 1890, lost in 1915. *From Lubbock's* The Down Easters, *1930.*

Operated by her builders, *Shenandoah* was largely employed in the California grain trade, carrying a crew of four officers and about thirty-five men. The *Shenandoah* was a good carrier, which made good passages at a time when the wooden sailing ship was nearly done. Her most famous commander was Captain James Murphy.

The big Down Easter had many notable events in her career, perhaps the most unusual coming during her passage around Cape Horn in 1898, when, among the icebergs, a meteor sailed overhead, a beautiful green color with a long tail of fire, subsequently hitting the water a short distance away.

Upon arriving in San Francisco in 1907 after a perilous voyage, the *Shenandoah* was laid up for over two years, finally sailing for New York in 1910 with a wide assortment of cargo, including scrap iron collected from the rubble of the 1906 San Francisco earthquake. This would prove to be her final voyage under sail, as she was sold for $36,000 and converted into a coal barge, her forest of masts and rigging removed. The final end of the *Shenandoah* came in 1915 when she was rammed and sunk by a steamship off Fire Island, New York, with one crewman lost.

ARYAN

Built by Charles Minnott at Phippsburg, Maine, in 1893, this 1,939-ton ship has the distinction of being the last wooden square-rigged ship ever built in the United States. One of her owners, a lawyer named Eugene Carver, the son of Searsport captain Nathan Carver, would be a major factor in keeping the *Aryan* in operation. With a distinctive white-painted hull (which was hell for her crew to upkeep), this attractive ship was largely employed in the California trade for most of her first twenty years in operation, often sailing in Dearborn & Co.'s Dispatch Line of clipper ships. While not a record-setter, she made most of her runs in good time, including a passage from Baltimore to San Francisco heavily laden with coal in 116 days in 1901. For the last four years of her career, from 1914 to 1918, the *Aryan* was employed in the Pacific. Historian Frederick Matthews commented, "Her being kept running was due to Mr. Carver's somewhat romantic ideas which it was said were not to his financial advantage." During this time, the ship was the only American square-rigged wooden ship still in operation. Many of her later runs were in the Pacific lumber trade, the ship making a fine passage in heavy weather from Vancouver to South Africa in 1914. The *Aryan*, the last of her type, met her end just before Christmas in 1918 while bound from Wellington, New Zealand, to San Francisco. The cargo caught fire some eight hundred miles from Wellington, and her crew was forced to abandon

The last square-rigger built in America, the *Aryan* came down the ways in Phippsburg, Maine, in 1893. *From Lubbock's* The Down Easters, *1930.*

ship in three lifeboats, the men watching helplessly as the flames toppled her masts. The boats subsequently made a course for the Chatham Islands, with two arriving safely, while one lifeboat with nine men was lost at sea.

DIRIGO

This aptly named ship, carrying the Maine state motto *Dirigo* (which means "I direct") on her stern, was the first steel-hulled sailing ship ever built in America. Put over by Arthur Sewall & Co. of Bath in 1894, this four-masted bark measured 3,005 tons, was 312 feet long and carried 13,000 yards of canvas. Built at a cost of $157,000, the steel for *Dirigo* was imported from Scotland, as was her design. She was, as historian Basil Lubbock states, "a typical British four-master of the nineties." The Sewalls would go on to build other steel sailing ships in order to keep their shipbuilding business afloat, employing immigrant shipbuilders from England and Scotland who knew this specialized trade, and while the last-ditch effort was a noble one, it

The first steel ship built in America, *Dirigo* was sunk by a German submarine in World War I. *From Lubbock's* The Down Easters, *1930.*

failed. Even these steel ships, starting with *Dirigo*, were expensive to operate and could not keep the same timetable as the modern steamships that had displaced sailing ships in most trades. The ship was first put in the case oil trade, making her maiden run from Philadelphia to Japan. On her second run from New York to San Francisco, *Dirigo* carried 4,500 tons of assorted cargo in the slow time of 153 days. The ship made other voyages to the Far East in the case oil trade, as well as carrying sugar from Honolulu and coal from Baltimore and other ports. Writer Jack London would even make a voyage from San Francisco to New York in *Dirigo* in about 1899, using some of the experience he gained for his 1904 book *The Sea-Wolf*.

Dirigo, like many a sailing ship, met her end during World War I. She carried a load of barley from Seattle for Sweden in October 1915 but was subsequently stopped by a British patrol ship, having received information that the cargo had been purchased by a German agent, with the intent that the ship would be "captured" by the Germans once she entered the Kattegat Strait between Sweden and Denmark. The cargo of the *Dirigo* was subsequently confiscated by the British, and the steel sailing ship was condemned as a war prize and subsequently sold to another American company, as ships were then in short supply. In May 1917, *Dirigo* made her final voyage, departing New York for Le Havre, France, but was stopped by the German submarine *UB-23* on May 31 six miles south of the Eddystone Light off the Cornish coast and subsequently sunk by explosives.

Chapter 9

SCHOONERS AND THE LAST DAYS
OF SAIL, 1871–PRESENT

*I*n addition to the square-riggers, the schooners of the American merchant fleet also played a vital role in our commerce, moving a wide variety of goods, many of them bulk cargoes like granite and coal, from ports all along the Atlantic coast, from Baltimore to Maine. The handy schooner, defined by its distinctive fore-and-aft rig, had played a vital part in American shipping since colonial times and would effectively be the last type of sailing ship used on a commercially viable basis until steam and motor vessels entirely eclipsed sailing vessels by the end of World War I.

The earliest coasting schooners were small in size, usually under one hundred tons, and were two-masted, carrying a modest sail plan. However, just as with the square-riggers, as American commerce expanded, so, too, did the size of the schooners over the years, thus enabling them to carry larger cargoes at a profitable rate. On average, a schooner required well under half the crew required of a similarly sized square-rigger. The other difference between the two types of sailing vessels were their areas of operations. With few exceptions, schooners were almost entirely employed in the coast-wise trade, carrying cargoes big and small from one port to another, capable of operating out of even the smallest New England ports due to their shallow draft. By the time the sailing ship era came to a close, schooners, though built in smaller numbers like all sailing ships, were also being built in massive sizes that the mariner of old would never have thought possible. The largest two-masted schooner was the 435-ton *Oliver Ames*, built in Massachusetts in 1866 for the coal trade. However, the three-masted schooner had by this time burst onto the scene. When these were first built is a matter of dispute, but by 1849, their building was well established. According to historian Paul C. Morris, only thirty-nine were registered by 1864, with only four of them over 500 tons.

Early on, two types of hull forms were used in these schooners. The shallow-draft type employed a centerboard (a retractable keel) projecting downward from the hull, which added stability and also made these so-called centerboarders quite fast. However, they could not carry as large a cargo as those schooners that had the hull of a regular square-rigger, so soon enough, a hull form was designed that incorporated the best of both worlds, resulting in a schooner that could carry a large cargo and was a good sailer. Though the three-masted schooner had her day, soon this type proved to be too small to carry a profitable cargo, and so the four-masted schooner came along in 1880. From that time forward, the schooners would rapidly advance in size. The first five-master was built in 1888 at Waldoboro, Maine, but as Morris recounts, "it was felt by many that the 'Gov. Ames' was a bit ahead of her time and it was not until 10 years after her launching that another five-master was built on the east coast." In 1899, when the first six-masted schooner was built, many folks thought that perhaps the limit had been reached in schooner building, and it largely was, though one seven-master was eventually built. Just as with the last of the square-rigged ships, there were schooners built with steel hulls, though not many. The most notable was the 2,128-ton *Kineo*, launched in 1903 and the last of the ships built at the Sewall shipyard in Bath, Maine.

While the building of such big schooners would continue, albeit in small numbers, after 1910, it was really the demand for shipping during World War I that quite literally kept what was left of the sailing shipbuilding industry afloat. With the advent of peace after 1918, that boom was over and the industry was gone for all practical purposes, though the last five-master was built in 1921, the last three-master in 1929 and the last of the old-time two-masted coasters in 1938. Despite the fact that the schooner was an economical vessel, other and even more inexpensive methods were found to transport bulk cargoes, most notably the barge. The coal industry was the last bastion of the great schooners until their ultimate demise. The later-day arrival of these behemoths to unload a cargo of that fossil fuel, which heated countless homes from the 1870s to the first decade of the twentieth century, was often the last opportunity for a large sailing vessel to be seen by the public in countless ports in New England. And when they were gone from the high seas, the only thing that remained of them were the hulks that

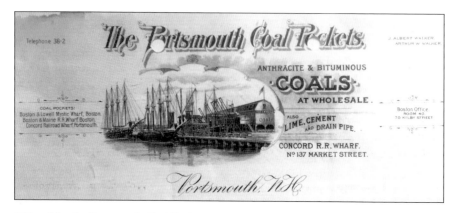

Billhead for the Portsmouth Coal Packets, one of many coal companies that employed schooners in New England. *Author's collection.*

floated, abandoned, in such ports as Providence, Boston, Boothbay Harbor and Wiscasset, until they, too, finally vanished. Luckily, the two-master has survived in small numbers. The oldest one in existence today, the *Lewis R. French*, operates as a windjammer out of Camden, Maine, and carries passengers in the summer months. Her billowing sails and fine form as she scuds across Penobscot Bay provide a picturesque reminder of a historic past that few can even imagine today.

LEWIS R. FRENCH

Built at Bristol, Maine, in 1871, this thirty-five-ton schooner was launched at Christmas Cove by the three sons of her namesake. Lewis French operated a dry goods store, and the vessel was subsequently employed as a coastal trader, bringing all types of goods back to Bristol to be sold in his store. Her first captain was Joseph French. However, the schooner—which had multiple owners who had a share in the schooner off and on over the years—was also employed in carrying other cargoes, including wood, bricks and the granite slabs that were used in the building trade. The *French*, which is about 101 feet long, 65 on the deck, and has a draft of 7 feet, is of very stout construction, including a double-sawn frame built of red oak and hackmatack, which made it possible to carry all manner of cargoes for years on end and still remain solid and seaworthy. The term "double sawn" refers to a traditional method of shipbuilding whereby the schooner has two constructed frames, one on top of the other, with the joints for each being at different points, thereby creating one thick frame, which is as close as a builder can get to one cut from a solid piece of timber.

After seven years, the *French* went into the fishing trade, employed in the menhaden fishery, until returning to the coastal trade in 1888. The *French* would remain in this trade, as she was originally rigged, until 1928, when she was converted to a motor vessel, her masts removed and a pilothouse built on her deck. From that time until 1973, the *French* was employed in the sardine cannery business, carrying sardine cargoes between Eastport, Maine, and New Brunswick, Canada.

At the age of 102, at a time when most others schooners had long ago disappeared, the *French* received a new life when new owner Captain John Foss of Rockland, Maine, restored her schooner rig and employed her in the windjammer trade beginning in 1976, carrying tourists in the summer months in Maine coastal waters. This trade got its start in 1936 as a way of saving some of the old Maine schooners and by the early 1950s was a booming business. It continues to this day as a way of preserving not only our national maritime heritage overall but especially that of Down East Maine. In 1986, Captain Foss sold the *French* to his brother-in-law Captain Dan Pease, who operated her in the same trade.

Today, this fine schooner is owned and operated by Captain Garth Wells and Captain Jenny Tobin, the vessel's four-person crew consisting of the captain, first mate, deckhand and cook. Both captains previously served as first mates in the windjammer fleet, with Captain Wells first aboard the *French* in 1998 as mate, after having spent some years aboard charter sailboats in the Caribbean. Tobin first gained her experience on the Great Lakes before eventually moving to Maine after gaining a wide variety of sailing experience on both the East and West Coasts, as well as in the Caribbean. Though the ship operates in old-time fashion, as Captain Wells comments, "we strike a balance between the modernizing of the schooner versus keeping it as old time as possible." While the U.S. Coast Guard of course insists on modern safety standards, the *French* only has an auxiliary motor, no inline engine, and has even been allowed to retain her kerosene running lights. As for the *French*'s three thousand yards of canvas sail, these are sewn by an experienced sailmaker in Boothbay Harbor—the same one who makes the sails for the USS *Constitution*. They are historically accurate and have a life of anywhere from ten to fifteen years. When asked about the historic side of operating the *French*, Captain Wells enthusiastically states, "When I'm steering while sailing, I'm doing exactly what the guy in 1871 was doing, and in the same

The schooner *Lewis R. French* under sail off the Owl's Head lighthouse on the Maine coast, July 2013. *Courtesy schooner* Lewis R. French.

area!" When handling the schooner, he says it just has an "old-time feel." In fact, this traditional way of doing things surprises many passengers, and Wells's ideal of "keeping it as clean as we can" really pays off. Of course, in the off-season, the upkeep of a schooner like the *French* can be an adventure. As Captain Wells recounts, "Every winter it's a new job" as the *Lewis R. French* is hauled out of the water, inspected and worked on for the following season, and Wells and Tobin have their hands full in both recruiting and training a crew, as well as keeping "everything running smoothly." To this day, you can take a cruise aboard the *French* in the summer months and take a hand in heaving up the anchor, handling the sails and even manning the helm. The *Lewis R. French*, having lived many varied lives, is significant as being the oldest two-masted schooner in the United States and the oldest surviving sailing ship built in the state of Maine. She is well worth a visit.

Governor Ames

Built at Waldoboro, Maine, by Leavitt Storer in 1888, the *Governor Ames* was designed by Albert Winslow of Taunton, Massachusetts. The ship was built for Captain Cornelius Davis of nearby Somerset, Massachusetts, and meant for the coal trade. This schooner is notable as the first oceangoing five-masted schooner ever built; a five-master was previously built on the Great Lakes in 1881. On her maiden voyage, she nearly met with disaster while bound empty from Waldoboro to Baltimore, as heavy weather caused the large 1,778-ton schooner to roll violently, causing her masts to go overboard while off Georges Bank. The *Ames* was subsequently anchored in place to ride out the storm and was then towed to Boston and rerigged at a cost of some $20,000. Because of this ill luck, the *Governor Ames* was considered an unsuccessful experiment, and it would not be until ten years later that another five-masted schooner was built. Despite this rough start, the *Ames* would recover and go on to have a useful and varied life. She first carried one of the largest cargoes of lumber ever at that time from Maine to Argentina, following which she carried lumber around Cape Horn to San Francisco in 1890, making the voyage in 143 days. Subsequently operating in the trans-Pacific lumber trade for four years before returning to the East Coast, the *Ames* was eventually put in the coal trade for which she was intended. Indeed, her career was more varied than that of most Maine-built schooners and seems to have been more mishap-filled on the East Coast. The *Governor Ames* sailed in the coal trade for about fifteen years before being grounded off the Florida Keys in 1899. The schooner met her end in December 1909 when bound from Brunswick, Georgia, with railroad ties. She was driven

The five-masted schooner *Governor Ames*, the first oceangoing ship of her kind, built in 1888. *From Parker's* Great Coal Schooners of New England, *1948.*

ashore onto Wimble Shoals off Cape Hatteras, North Carolina, during a heavy gale, and thirteen out of her fourteen crew and passengers, including the captain's wife, perished in the wreck.

George W. Wells

This schooner, famed as the first six-master, was built in Camden, Maine, at the shipyard of Holly Bean, one of the most prolific and famed schooner builders in New England. At her launching in August 1900, some ten thousand spectators witnessed the event and a flock of white pigeons was released as the *Wells* began to slide down the ways after her christening. This behemoth measured in at 2,970 tons and was 319 feet long, capable of carrying 5,000 tons of coal. Framed with white oak and spreading some twelve thousand yards of canvas, the schooner cost $120,000 to build, a huge investment for her owner, Captain John Crowley of Boston. Interestingly, her masts were made from Oregon pine, showing just how depleted the forests of Maine had become by this time. This schooner was also finely outfitted, equipped with staterooms paneled in cherry and furnished with hot and

Postcard view of the *George W. Wells*, the first six-masted schooner, built in 1900 by Holly Bean. *Author's collection.*

cold running water, electricity, heat and a telephone connected to the galley. Painted black with white trim, the *Wells* was a handsome vessel in every way but also a fast one, making the trip from Portland to the Virginia Capes in fifty-one hours in 1907. Her career was a successful one, though when less than a year old she collided with the only other six-master in existence, the *Eleanor A. Percy*, but neither was seriously damaged. The career of the *George W. Wells* was cut short in 1913. While bound from Boston to Fernandina, Florida, in September, the schooner ran into a hurricane and soon began to take on water. With her sails torn to pieces, she eventually drifted ashore at Ocracoke Inlet, North Carolina. Aided by the heroic efforts of surfmen from the Hatteras Inlet Lifesaving Station, eventually all twenty-six passengers and crew, as well as Captain Joseph York's St. Bernard dog, were eventually rescued and brought ashore after an ordeal that lasted hours. The wreck holds the distinction of being the largest ever of a sailing ship on the North Carolina coast, and remnants of the *Wells*'s hull, which was originally sold as salvage for $800 (the schooner was valued at $80,000 when lost) and later burned, are still visible today at times.

THOMAS W. LAWSON

This monumental vessel, the only seven-masted schooner ever to be built, is a famed one with a complicated legacy and a rather short career. Designed by B.B. Crowninshield, this steel-hulled schooner was built in 1901–2 at the Fore River Shipyard at Quincy, Massachusetts, for a consortium of owners that included her namesake, Thomas Lawson, a noted financier who was also interested in nautical affairs and wrote an early definitive history of the America's Cup the same year the *Lawson* was launched. This schooner, the first ever built of steel, was massive in size and was, in fact, the largest sailing vessel ever built, measuring in at 5,218 tons, 376 feet long, 50 feet in beam and a hold nearly 33 feet deep. She had a double bottom that allowed for over 1,000 tons of water ballast, her masts soared 150 feet above her deck, her bowsprit was 85 feet long and she carried over 44,000 yards of canvas. The *Lawson* could carry over 9,000 tons of coal. Because a seven-masted vessel had never been built before, a naming system for her masts had to be devised, but one was likely never settled on, and most likely her crew referred to them by number, though some have suggested that they were named after the days of the week.

The seven-masted schooner *Thomas W. Lawson*, built in 1901–2 at the Fore River Shipyard. *From Crowninshield's* Fore-and-Afters, *1940.*

Needless to say, this schooner was a one of a kind, and most evidence points to the fact that she could be difficult to handle in any but ideal conditions. As to her looks, well, though she certainly commanded attention, as historian Paul C. Morris states, "her high, unattractive bow…did little to enhance her already bulky looks and how anyone could call the 'Lawson' a pretty, or even a handsome vessel is beyond comprehension." On her first empty voyage from Boston to Philadelphia, designer Crowninshield took passage on his creation and experienced firsthand how difficult she was to handle.

The *Thomas W. Lawson* operated in the coal trade for several years, but when freight rates fell below sixty cents a ton and the waits at coal docks grew longer—as much as two months—due to strikes at coal mines, the great schooner was no longer economically viable. As a result, in 1906, the *Lawson* was converted into an oil tanker at the Newport News Shipyard in Virginia and subsequently leased to the Sun Oil Company, her hull divided into fourteen tanks and able to carry some 2,450,000 gallons of oil. At this time, her masts were also cut down in size, and the big schooner was largely towed to her destinations rather than sailing on her own. She would not last long in this trade. Chartered to the Standard Oil Company in 1907, the *Thomas W. Lawson* was sent on a transatlantic voyage in November 1907, bound from Marcus Hook, Pennsylvania, to England carrying over two million gallons of oil worth $71,000. Manned by a crew of eighteen men, the large schooner soon encountered hurricane-strength winds and had her sails blown away but plodded on her way, eventually making landfall, though off course, off the Scilly Islands on December 13. Though a pilot had come aboard the *Lawson* and a lifeboat from the St. Agnes Station offered assistance, the schooner's captain declined any help. However, he soon changed his mind when a severe gale sprang up, but it was too late. The ship was battered for several hours until, just after 1:00 a.m., her anchor broke and the *Lawson* was at the mercy of the sea. Lifejackets were donned by the crew and flares sent into the night sky. Just after 2:30 a.m., the *Lawson* met her end when the giant schooner was blown on the rocks of the aptly named Hellweather Reef, subsequently breaking in two and rolling over to sink in deep water. Two men, including Captain George Dow, survived the sinking, but the once-mighty schooner was gone. Though by almost every measure the ship was an economic failure, the *Lawson* remains an important milestone in American and New England shipbuilding, a last-gasp effort to keep the era of the sailing ship alive.

Wyoming

Measuring in at 3,730 tons and 450 feet long, the *Wyoming* has the distinction of being not just the largest and last six-masted schooner ever built but also the largest wooden ship ever to sail the seas. She was built at a cost of $190,000 in 1909 by Percy & Small in Bath, Maine, a prominent shipyard that employed some two hundred men and was known for the seven six-masters that it built between 1902 and 1909. Owned by a group of men that included her builders and the governor of Wyoming, the schooner was named after the state because of that notable western investor and others. The schooner was homeported out of Bath and intended for the coal trade, making her maiden voyage under Captain Angus MacLeod to Newport News, Virginia, to load that cargo to the tune of over 6,000 tons.

Despite her size and large building cost, the *Wyoming* was a very profitable vessel. In 1916, she was chartered to the International Paper Company and the following year was sold to the newly formed France & Canada Steamship Company for the reported price of $350,000, for the purpose of shipping vital commodities to war-torn France. After the war, in 1919, the *Wyoming*

The Maine-built six-masted schooner *Wyoming*, the largest wooden ship ever built. She was built in 1909 at Bath and lost off Nantucket in 1924. *Courtesy Library of Congress.*

returned to the coal trade, carrying under charter a large cargo of black diamonds from Virginia to Genoa, Italy. In 1921, the schooner was again sold, this time to Captain A.W. Frost & Company of Portland, Maine, still employed in the coal trade.

The great schooner *Wyoming* would meet her end in March 1924 while bound from Norfolk, Virginia, to St. John, New Brunswick, with a load of coal. While caught in a blizzard in Nantucket Sound, off Chatham, Massachusetts, the schooner dropped anchor with another schooner, the five-masted *Cora F. Cressey*. While the smaller schooner survived the storm, the *Wyoming* disappeared with her fourteen-man crew, likely foundering near the Pollock Rip Lightship. Until wreckage with her name on it washed ashore, what had become of the *Wyoming* was a mystery and would remain so for years, many believing that possibly the heavily laden schooner struck bottom during the storm. In 2003, the wreckage of the great schooner was located, with surveys showing that the *Wyoming* was badly broken amidships, lending credence to the idea that she struck bottom and quickly took on water.

LUTHER LITTLE AND HESPER

Considered separately, neither of these four-masted schooners, both built in Somerset, Massachusetts, had a long or prosperous career that makes them notable examples, nor were the details of their construction or building anything outside the ordinary. However, together, these two otherwise ordinary schooners would turn out to be unlikely survivors, the final representatives of the great schooners that were built in New England. They were viewed by millions of tourists who made their way to coastal Maine from 1932 until their final demise in 1998. Once they were gone, so, too, was any substantial physical representation of these great ships.

The first of these schooners built was the *Luther Little*, measuring 1,234 tons, built by the Read Brothers in 1917. Her active sailing career would last about eight years in the coastal trade, carrying cargoes of coal and lumber and sailing as far south as Haiti, where she grounded in 1920. Probably the most important or exciting event in her career came in June 1918. While sailing off the coast of Delaware, the ship and crew rescued two balloonists from the Naval Station at Cape May, New Jersey, who had crashed into the sea. However, by 1925, the ship was out of business and laid up.

As for the *Hesper*, she was built by the noted Crowninshield Shipbuilding Company, which established its yard in South Somerset, Massachusetts, in about 1917. This schooner was believed to be their first vessel before they turned to building oceangoing tugboats for the United States Shipping Board. The 1,348-ton schooner was unlucky from the very start, being grounded as she slid down the builder's ways on her launching day, July 4, 1918, and stuck there for two weeks before finally taking to the water—never a good start for a vessel. This schooner was designed by yard foreman E.J. Blinn for Rogers & Webb of Boston. The ship had an oak frame and yellow pine decking and could carry up to 2,000 tons of cargo. This schooner ventured across the Atlantic to Spain and also as far south as Venezuela during her brief career, and she grounded in Boston Harbor in 1925, requiring the assistance of tugs to be freed. However, her career was nearly at an end, and by 1927, she was laid up at Rockport, Maine. There, more bad luck followed when she broke free from her moorings and was beached during a storm in January 1928. She was eventually freed yet again and eventually sailed to Portland, where she continued to be out of service.

Both schooners would see potential new life in 1932, when they were purchased by a man named Frank Winter and towed to Wiscasset, Maine. He paid but $600 for the *Hesper* and acquired the *Luther Little* at auction.

The Wiscasset schooners, *Hesper* (*at left*) and *Luther Little*, in port since 1932, as they appeared in the 1990s. *Author's collection.*

However, once these schooners arrived at Wiscasset, they were never sent to sea again. Winter had purchased the schooners, as well as the defunct Wiscasset, Waterville & Farmington narrow-gauge railroad, as part of a moneymaking scheme, the plan being for the railroad to transport lumber to Wiscasset, where the two schooners would take the cargo south for sale, returning with coal, both trades for which these vessels were well suited. However, before the business was up and running, Winter died, and with the nation now in a full-scale depression, so did his plans for the newly acquired schooners. Thus, they lay where they were berthed, and there they would stay for the next sixty-eight years. The sight of moored and abandoned schooners was once common in New England ports and harbors, but over the years, the *Luther Little* and *Hesper* would become the last, somehow surviving time and tide. Even by 1940, the ships were unseaworthy without some major repairs. B.B. Crowninshield commented in 1940 about the one that his company built, "Since 1936 the tide has ebbed and flowed through her hull in a Down East harbor." It was not just time and the elements that took their toll; so, too, did deliberate vandalism. The *Hesper*'s masts were cut down in 1940, while her aft wheelhouse was burned in 1945 to celebrate the end of World War II. Her forward wheelhouse would survive until it, too, was burned in 1978. The ships were also scarred by numerous small fires over the years, most likely set by vandals.

But despite all of this abuse, the schooners remained. Indeed, the *Luther Little* and *Hesper* became a popular tourist attraction along busy U.S. Route 1, the subject of many paintings and photographs over the years as they retained their form throughout the 1980s. During the 1930s and 1940s, when the age of sail was yet to be fully documented or appreciated at a local level, the schooners were likely considered more of a nuisance than anything, but by the 1960s, their status would change. By this time, they were the only surviving schooners anywhere in New England, and despite their slow decay, they were now a real attraction. Just why the schooners were never fully preserved until their condition made such a proposition unviable is a fair question to ask. Anecdotal evidence, including discussions with locals, leads me to believe that because these ships had been essentially hauled here and then abandoned, there was no personal connection to the town so there was no real interest in them. Add to this the fact that they were not Maine-built vessels, but rather ones built in Massachusetts, and they were deemed even more unworthy of preservation. Had these schooners been built in Maine, one or both of them might have been subject to serious preservation efforts, but this was not the case. Interestingly, preservation efforts were discussed in about 1965, focusing on the *Luther Little*, as the *Hesper* had already been stripped and vandalized, but these efforts never gained traction. An organization called the Friends of the Wiscasset Schooners, as they had come to be called, was formed in 1978, but their efforts at preservation also came to naught after the *Little*'s rear mast went overboard during a small earthquake in 1979. In 1980, the stern quarter collapsed and sank into the mud.

The ships lay as they were for decades, but by the 1990s, they were on their last legs. The *Hesper*'s hull gave up the ghost in 1990, finally collapsing and leaving nothing but a large pile of wood debris after a storm, while during a storm in 1995, the *Luther Little*'s three remaining masts went by the way and her hull rapidly disintegrated. By 1998, little was left but a sodden pile of wood debris, and thus it was that the now unsightly mess was hauled away, though some recognizable components were saved. With that, the *Luther Little* and *Hesper* were gone forever. The components of these schooners remain in storage to this day, with plans for a small waterfront museum yet to come to fruition, but one mystery remains concerning the ship's seven-ton anchors. Some believe that they were sold for scrap during World War II, but others believe they were removed when the schooners were moved to their final position and subsequently dumped in the Sheepscot River and that they are still out there somewhere, awaiting rediscovery.

Chapter 10

STEAMSHIPS, 1793–1950

*T*he age of the steamship as an economically viable form of waterborne transport got its start in America in 1807 with New Yorker Robert Fulton and his famed vessel the *North River Steamboat* (often referred to erroneously as the *Clermont*). However, the steamship built by Fulton and financed by his powerful partner Robert Livingston was not the first such vessel to be built. James Watt of Scotland had invented the most modern steam engine, based on the prior work of English inventor Thomas Newcomen and his "atmospheric" engine. Because of the recent American Revolution, however, Watt's technology could not be imported to America. No matter, for inventor John Fitch, a native of Windsor, Connecticut, now living in Philadelphia, having seen a drawing of Newcomen's engine and aware of Watt's work, developed an engine of his own that he used to power his steamboat, the *Perseverance*, up and down the Delaware River beginning in August 1787. A strange but successful craft, this boat did not employ a paddlewheel but rather employed steam-powered oars. This momentous event occurred during the historic time when the Constitutional Convention was being held in Philadelphia, so Fitch's boat carried many passengers up and down the Delaware River that summer, among them Benjamin Franklin. Unfortunately, while Fitch was granted a patent for his invention in 1791, it was not as broad as he would have liked, and he had competitors, with the result that though his boat was a good one, Fitch did not have the resources to make it commercially successful. The practical success in the steamboat business fell to Robert Fulton, a notable inventor to be sure, but one with the advantage of wealth and a powerful backer. Moreover, since the early history of the steamboat centered on operations on the Delaware and Hudson Rivers, it was in this area that the building of steamships—first made of wood and, later, iron—would become centered. While, eventually, important steamships would come to be built in New England by the late nineteenth century, New York and Delaware River–area builders remained predominant. In fact, by the early 1850s, during the clipper ship era, while New England would turn out hundreds of wooden sailing ships, New York shipyards were already turning to the future and steamships.

The one New England state that got an early start in steamship building was Connecticut. Its two pioneer vessels were the small *John Hancock* and the *Eagle*, both built at Norwich by Gilbert Brewster in 1817. The latter boat was built for the Nantasket Beach Steamboat Company and plied the waters of Boston Bay until being broken up in 1824. Massachusetts would soon follow suit and build some small steamships on the Merrimack River as early as 1818. Even when steamship building did start, it was often the case that, as with the *Kennebec*, which sailed the Maine coast in the early 1820s, they were crudely built and underpowered, or the hull was built locally but the engines were supplied by New York or Pennsylvania engine builders. For those steamships that were built in New England, most were small in size, under 100 tons, and such cities as New York, Philadelphia, Wilmington, Cleveland and Buffalo alone built more steamships than all of New England combined. Even by 1888, there were only thirteen steamships in American registry that measured from 500 to 1,000 tons and only sixteen over 1,000 tons that were built in New England. The state of Connecticut would maintain its predominance in New England into the early twentieth century, with Noank and Mystic being notable building centers for steamships, though many smaller boats were also built early on the Connecticut River. Interestingly, two such Connecticut River boats—the 1835-built *Bunker Hill* of 356 tons and the 1838-built *Charter Oak* of 440 tons—were built at New Haven and later transported to the Maine coast and began operations there in 1844. Bath, Maine, was also an important building center for steamships, while the Boston area was a distant third, though some big ships were built there.

Nearly all of these vessels sailed in established lines, usually associated with major railroads that provided regular passenger and freight service between New York, Boston, Portland and a number of other ports both in between and beyond. Perhaps the most famous and long-lasting was the Fall River Line, which operated from 1847 to 1937 between Fall River, Massachusetts, and New York City. Most of its well-known and popular passenger steamers were built in New York, but its big freight boat, the 2,533-ton *City of Fall River*, was built at Chelsea, Massachusetts. Other notable steamship lines include the Maine Steamship Line between New York and Portland, the Metropolitan Steamship Line between Boston and New York (later the Eastern Steamship Company), the Providence and New York Steamship Company and the Norwich and New York Transportation Company, to name just a few. The most long-lived of these steamship lines would operate into the years leading up to World War II, eventually put out of business due to the quick growth of auto transportation.

While most of our attention is here placed on oceangoing steamships, by the late nineteenth century, steamships were also being operated on smaller New England rivers and, most notably, to serve the burgeoning tourist trade on large lakes, carrying tens of thousands of passengers a year. New England's three largest lakes—Lake Champlain in Vermont, Lake Winnipesaukee in New Hampshire and Moosehead Lake in Maine—each had notable steamers plying their waters. This is another instance where the class of these ships as a whole is greater than the sum of the individual ships. None of these lake steamers was of unique or unusual design, nor were their exploits or feats of freshwater sailing overly noteworthy. However, as a group these ships, representative of some of the finest and most popular in their respective regions, were very important, a real boom to the tourist economy and trade, but also added the intangible qualities of joy and fond memories to all who trod their decks in the summer months, causing many passengers to return time after time, year after year. Indeed, as the resident of a Lake Winnipesaukee port city for many years, I have personally experienced and witnessed the impact one of these vessels has continued to have on the region, and it never fails to amaze me.

PORTLAND

The sinking of the grand liner RMS *Titanic* in the North Atlantic shocked the world in April 1912, but for New Englanders, it served as a somber reminder of an earlier sinking in 1898 that claimed a great loss of life and shocked the region to its core. The steamship *Portland*, a side-wheel paddle steamer, was built at Bath, Maine, in 1889 by the New England Shipbuilding Co. at a cost of $250,000. She was a large vessel for her day, weighing in at 2,284 tons and 291 feet long, fitted out to carry seven hundred passengers, powered by a 1,200-horsepower vertical beam steam engine manufactured at the Bath Iron Works. She was a popular passenger steamer in her day, and during her years of operation, she carried hundreds of thousands of passengers between Portland and Boston's India Wharf. As she was beautifully outfitted, both in form and in her well-appointed staterooms, voyaging on the *Portland* during the twenty-four-hour run between Portland and Boston was the height of luxury.

At 7:00 p.m. on November 26, 1898, just two days after Thanksgiving, the *Portland* departed Boston under the command of Captain Hollis Blanchard. Many of the passengers were returning home after the holiday. However, while two storm systems were heading toward the Massachusetts coast, Blanchard knew of only one and told a fellow captain that he could beat the storm to Portland, Maine. While the general manager of the steamship line ordered its ships to delay their sailing until 9:00 p.m., Blanchard sailed anyway. Maybe he didn't get the order to delay, or perhaps he ignored it—we can never know. Legend has it that one passenger saw a mother cat carrying her kittens off the ship and thereby decided that maybe she knew something he didn't and decided to disembark. Call it superstition or whatever you will, the decision saved his life. The *Portland* was seen at

Drawing of the *Portland*, lost in a gale in 1898, by Samuel Ward Stanton, who was lost on the *Titanic*. *From Stanton's* American Steam Ships, *1895*.

sea by several vessels after her departure and was last seen near Thatcher's Island off Gloucester, damaged and with her running lights extinguished, just before midnight. The steamship was never seen afloat again, and by 7:00 p.m. on November 27, the bodies of some of her passengers began coming ashore at Provincetown on Cape Cod. Only 36 bodies were ever recovered; the rest were swallowed up by the deep ocean. Estimates vary as to how many people were lost, as the passenger list went down with the steamer, but modern estimates range between 192 and 245 individuals, including the *Portland*'s 63-man crew. The storm in which she was lost soon became known as the Portland Gale after its most famous victim and is still famed today for its ferocity. The monster storm, which spawned a ten-foot storm surge in some areas, killed over 400 people and resulted in the sinking of over 150 vessels.

The sinking of the *Portland* also, sadly, signaled the end of an era, as paddlewheel steamers were rapidly being replaced by propeller-driven ships. It was not until 2002 that the ghost of the *Portland* was discovered. The wreck was located by divers in over four hundred feet of water seven miles off the coast of Massachusetts in the Stellwagen Bank National Marine Sanctuary and subsequently listed in the National Register of Historic Places in 2005. Though this tragedy, New England's own version of the *Titanic*, took place over one hundred years ago, it remains a part of New England lore and legend and still ranks high among the regional disasters in terms of lives lost.

CITY OF LOWELL

Nicknamed the "Greyhound of the Sound" from the very first, this notable steamship was just the eighth ship built by Maine's Bath Iron Works, established in 1884. This steamer, built for the Norwich and New York Transportation Company in 1893–94, measured in at 2,975 tons, was 337 feet long and could accommodate just over six hundred passengers and carry over 100,000 cubic feet of freight. She was manned with a crew of about one hundred and was powered by several triple-expansion steam engines fed by six huge boilers that required 90 tons of coal for each round trip between New York and New London, Connecticut. The two four-bladed propellers that drove this steamer through the water were huge, having a diameter of some 11 feet. From the get-go, this steamer was fast, reaching speeds of nineteen knots in her first voyages.

Postcard view of the steamship *City of Lowell*, known as the "Greyhound of the Sound," built at Bath, Maine, 1893–94. *Author's collection.*

Not only was the *City of Lowell* fast, she was also well appointed with first-class staterooms and even some "bridal chambers." Common areas included a dining hall that offered a simple dinner for seventy-five cents, a café, a social hall and a section amidships that offered passengers a look into the engine room. Schedules show that the trip each way was made in just under twelve hours, with subsequent rail connections in New England to Worcester and Boston. Sometimes called a "night boat" for the overnight runs she made in quick time, the *City of Lowell* was among the best ships of her era. For wealthier businessmen or families, a trip aboard the *City of Lowell* might be a regular occurrence, but for many others, a journey aboard such a ship was the trip of a lifetime.

The *City of Lowell* operated in this line for over forty years, the line changing names a number of times over the years, last known as the New England Steamship Company from 1912 to 1939. The ship seems to have been not only popular but lucky as well. A frequent visitor to the busy harbor of New York, she was largely free of mishaps, except for a collision with the ferry *Columbia* while sailing on the East River in heavy fog in November 1904. However, all good things must come to an end, and in 1938, the *City of Lowell* was laid up, scheduled to go to the shipbreakers after a long life. Waiting to be scrapped, the ship was subsequently transferred to the War Shipping Administration in 1942 and sold to the War Department in 1943 for use as a barracks ship in Brooklyn, New York. After the war, the steamer finally met her end when she was broken up sometime after 1946.

Minnesota and Dakota

It's hard to believe, but in 1903, the two largest steamships ever built in the United States up to that time were launched in New London, Connecticut, by the Eastern Shipbuilding Company. This company just the year before had become part of the United States Shipbuilding Company, a consortium of six large, previously independent shipbuilding companies. The sister ships *Minnesota* and *Dakota* were built for railroad magnate James Hill of Minnesota and his Great Northern Steamship Company, which operated between Seattle and the Far East. Together, they cost just over $7.8 million to build. While the ship was manned by American officers, many of the crew were Chinese.

It would take over three years to complete the ships and get them to sea. They were laid down in 1901, with the *Minnesota* being launched in April 1903. She measured in at 20,718 tons, was 622 feet long, was powered by two triple-expansion engines capable of a speed of fourteen knots and could carry a huge cargo equal to that of 2,500 railroad cars, as well as having nine decks to accommodate up to 2,600 passengers (most in the lower steerage compartment). The *Dakota* was launched in February 1904 and was almost identical in size, except for measuring 4 tons less. The ships were said to be the most luxuriously appointed vessels of the day, and hopes were high for their operations. However, though they were well built and impressive, the ships would never turn a profit.

The *Dakota*, which made her maiden voyage beginning in April 1905, departing New York for Seattle with a general cargo that included six thousand tons of steel rails for the Alaska Railroad, would have a short life. On her second voyage, she departed Seattle for Yokohama, Japan, carrying a cargo of nineteen locomotives and one hundred railroad cars, as well as that country's peace delegation that signed the treaty ending the Russo-Japanese War. However, she met her end on just her seventh voyage while bound to Tokyo in March 1907, her negligent captain driving her hard aground on a reef while running at top speed. While the crew were saved, the stranded ship was abandoned to the insurance company. James Hill was compensated $2.5 million for the vessel and her cargo. The ship was initially thought to be salvageable, but as she was stranded in a precarious position, storms later that month caused the *Dakota* to break into two and sink.

As for the *Minnesota*, she was more fortunate in her fate but never turned a profit either on her total of forty voyages over the years. This ship, too, was initially employed in the trade with the Far East, carrying grain out to Asia and returning with the time-honored Chinese imports of silk and

Postcard view of the steamer *Minnesota*, the largest steamship ever built in the United States when launched in 1903 in Connecticut. *Author's collection.*

other fabrics, as well as passengers. However, the *Minnesota* was much too big and always had trouble loading a full cargo and, with her astronomical fuel costs, was a huge money burner instead. The ship gained new life with the strong demand for shipping in World War I so was shifted to operations in the North Atlantic in 1915 and subsequently chartered by the British. However, sabotaged by German nationals in her crew, she was tied up in repairs and legal disputes for over a year before being sold in 1917 for $2.6 million. She would subsequently make seven round trips between U.S. East Coast ports and England during the war, armed with a deck gun manned by a naval crew. In 1919, the U.S. Navy chartered the *Minnesota* as a troop ship and renamed her the USS *Troy*; she made three voyages to bring American troops home. After this duty was over, she was returned to her owners but would never sail again, subsequently being sold for scrap metal and broken up in Germany in 1923—an ignominious end for what was once the largest and grandest ship in the entire American merchant marine.

THE LAKES STEAMERS MOUNT WASHINGTON, TICONDEROGA AND KATAHDIN

Three surviving lake boats are excellent representatives of this kind of steamship. Two of them are still operating, while the third has been preserved and sits on dry land not far from the place where she first took to the water. The boat with the longest history is the *Mount Washington*, which sails on New Hampshire's Lake Winnipesaukee. She was built as a replacement for the original "*Mount*," a paddlewheel steamer that was built by the Boston & Maine Railroad and operated from 1872 until she caught fire and burned in 1939. Very soon after, a new company was formed to build a new *Mount Washington*. That company purchased the old iron hull of the steamer *Chateaugay*, which was built in 1888 and sailed for years on Lake Champlain before the steamer was turned into a floating clubhouse for the Burlington Yacht Club in Vermont. The iron hull was cut into twenty pieces and transported to Lakeport, New Hampshire, and used as the basis for the new *Mount Washington* that was built there by the Boston General Ship & Engine Works and launched in 1940. Since that time, the *Mount* has been in continual use on Lake Winnipesaukee, with Weirs Beach (Laconia) being her homeport and her ports of call on the lake being Wolfeboro, Alton Bay, Meredith Bay and Center Harbor. The two original engines of the *Mount* built in 1940 came from an oceangoing yacht but were given over to the U.S. Navy in World War II. After the war, the *Mount* was fitted with two new Enterprise diesel engines and in 2010 was re-engined with two new Caterpillar C32 V-12 marine diesel engines. The ship (as she is now designated) has also been lengthened over the years and is now 230 feet long and can carry 1,250 passengers. The *Mount* has been a popular vessel since the end of the war and remains so to this day. Her passengers are offered a chance to enjoy the big lake just as tourists did over one hundred years ago. While the *Mount* is put out of service in the late fall before the lake freezes over for the winter, those who live around the lake wait for the day, usually in April, when "ice out" is declared. This event heralds the time when the *Mount* will once again be making her ports of call.

Our next notable ship in this group is the *Ticonderoga*, which first hit the waters of Lake Champlain at Shelburne, Vermont, in 1906. This 892-ton, 220-foot-long steamer, powered by a vertical beam engine, was built by the Champlain Transportation Company. She was assembled and launched at the Shelburne Shipyard, her hull having been fashioned in Newburgh, New York. The *Ticonderoga* carried both freight and passengers first between Westport, New York, and St. Albans, Vermont, but would also run between Burlington and Port Kent, New York. The boat was a popular and important part of Lake Champlain life, carrying freight of all kinds, including farm produce and even cattle, as well as pleasure and business travelers. During both world wars, the *Ticonderoga* also ferried army troops across the lake. Though she had her fair share of minor mishaps, the *Ticonderoga* was a very

Above: The Lake Winnipesaukee ship *Mount Washington*, known as "the Mount," at dockside in Center Harbor, New Hampshire. *Author photo.*

Opposite, top: Postcard view of the Lake Champlain steamer *Ticonderoga*, built at Shelburne, Vermont, in 1906. *Author's collection.*

Opposite, bottom: Postcard view of the Moosehead Lake steamer *Katahdin*, built at Bath, Maine, and assembled at Greenville, 1914. *Author's collection.*

profitable steamer for years. However, with the advent of newer and faster boats on the lake, she eventually became obsolete, though remaining in operation as an excursion boat and even a floating casino for a time. The *Ticonderoga*, with the threat of being broken up, was sold in 1950 to socialite and noted antiques collector Electra Havemeyer Webb at the urging of Vermont writer and historian Ralph Nading Hill. Webb had just a few years before established the Shelburne Museum as a way of preserving objects of early American history, and the boat fit right in with her preservation ideals. While Webb tried keeping the *Ticonderoga* in operation, she had a tough time doing so, with high maintenance and the increasing difficulty in gaining a crew qualified to run what was now an antique. The boat made her last run in 1954, subsequently being transported overland to the grounds of the Shelburne Museum in 1955, with the elaborate interior restored to its original condition in the succeeding years. In 1964, the *Ticonderoga* was listed as a National Historic Landmark and to this day can still be seen on the grounds of the Shelburne Museum. Though high and dry on land, the steamer is very well maintained and is quite the sight to see. One is easily able to imagine her in her glory days traveling across Lake Champlain.

Our final boat under consideration here is the *Katahdin*, a steamer built in 1914 at the Bath Iron Works in Maine. This 120-ton, 102-foot-long steel-

hulled steamer was the sixty-third vessel built by the famed company best known for its naval ships and is significant as the oldest surviving ship built by that group. The *Katahdin*, named after Maine's Mount Katahdin, had a relatively short initial career as a passenger boat. She was built for the Coburn Steamship Company, which had the boat shipped in sections to Greenville, Maine. There she was reassembled and launched on Moosehead Lake and served as a tourist and packet boat on the lake for the next 24 years. Not only did the *Katahdin* offer pleasure cruises on the lake, but she also delivered passengers and supplies to the Mount Kineo Resort, able to carry about three hundred passengers at a time. Steamship service on Moosehead Lake had gotten its start in 1836, but just over 100 years later, in September 1938, the *Katahdin* made the last excursion trip on the lake. By the 1930s, the boat was no longer a moneymaker due to declining patronage, it being a period when the increasing use of the automobile changed the tourism trade forever. Laid up for several years, in 1940 the *Katahdin* was purchased by a local paper and pulp company, a huge industry in northern Maine, and was cut down to a towboat. She was used to haul pulpwood across the lake for over 30 years. This part of her career ended in 1976, after which she was laid up for several years until eventually acquired by the Moosehead Marine Museum. Her pleasure cruises on the lake would resume again after the *Katahdin* was gotten into shape, but it would not be until 2000 that she was fully restored to her original condition, a project that cost about $500,000 and took 5 years. Today, like other lake boats in New England, the "*Kate*" sails in the summer months from June into October, offering a wide variety of excursion trips and carrying on a tradition begun on Moosehead Lake over 180 years ago.

Chapter 11

ADVENTURE CRAFT AND SPORTING YACHTS, 1877–1899

Although all our notable ships previously discussed were working vessels, there were many smaller types of sailing vessels built that were also used for recreational purposes. Boating for pleasure has taken place in American waters for hundreds of years, even if formal boating clubs were not established until the early 1800s. Such boats used for this purpose, if propelled by sail, were usually smaller fore-and-aft rigged vessels that came in many different types, such as a sloop, yawl, ketch, cutter or catboat, depending on the configuration of their sail plans. Most had one mast and are distinct relations to the schooner. Such craft as this were also employed in a wide variety of trades, whether it be fishing, oystering or the coastal trade, and were built for those purposes, but also in their owners' off-hours were used for sport and pleasure. By the 1830s in America, there were some sailing ships that were built solely for sport and leisure, not as working boats in the traditional dual-purpose role. Indeed, all of the vessels in this chapter, out of all proportion to their size, made waves in the mind of the American public in the late nineteenth century. The sailing ship era for large commercial ships was drawing to a close when our examples were making people take notice, but the small sailing craft that they represent are timeless in helping mankind to maintain our intimate connection with the sea. Our first vessels in this category were sailed by true master mariners and adventurers, men who understood the ways of the sea and were not afraid to push things to the limit. While there is no evidence that Captain Thomas Crapo and Captain Joshua Slocum ever met in person or even knew each other, they nonetheless would have understood each other very well.

New Bedford

This odd and seaworthy vessel was designed by seaman Thomas Crapo of New Bedford, Massachusetts, and was built by Samuel Mitchell at his boat-building shop on Fish Island in the Acushnet River. This craft, which was described alternatively as a whaleboat with a schooner rig or a dory, was similar in size to that type of mast-less fishing boat at nineteen feet, seven inches long, just over six feet wide and thirty inches deep, with a draft of just thirteen inches when fully loaded. However, this "boat" had two masts, each twenty-one feet tall and was fore-and-aft rigged with a triangular sail nicknamed a "leg of mutton," the whole comprising just twenty-five yards of light duck canvas sailcloth. The craft was also decked over to provide shelter and had two hatchways, one forward and one aft.

Crapo, born in 1842 in New Bedford, led an adventurous life at sea for many years but in 1876 found himself back on dry land, employed at a junk shop. This the old sailor found disagreeable, so he soon turned to an idea he had had for years, that of crossing the Atlantic Ocean in a small boat. The full details of Crapo's adventures, recounted in his autobiography, are well worth reading. He wrote in his book *Strange but True*, "I was venturesome and daring and I thought if I could manage to eclipse all others I could make considerable money by doing so." With this in mind, Crapo drew up plans for his boat and took them to a well-known whaleboat builder to build his craft. Once she was completed in mid-May 1877, the boat, which weighed but five hundred pounds empty, was taken by Crapo and stored away. He subsequently gave notice to his employer. Within a day or so, word got out about Crapo's plans to cross the Atlantic and caused quite a stir, some judging him to be perhaps a bit crazy. Crapo had planned on his boat, called the *New Bedford*, to carry but one person, himself, but he was in for an awakening. His wife, Joanna, anxious about the voyage, resolved that she would accompany her husband on the trip and that nothing would dissuade her from that notion. Crapo would later lament that, had he known she was coming along, he would have planned for a larger boat, but such are the plans of men who fail to confide to their wives in advance! In fairness to Crapo, he acknowledged his wife as one who had "proven herself an accomplished sailor," and he accepted her decision "as coolly as possible," and so it was done. Interestingly, regarding reports on his character or sanity, Crapo stated, "Very few husbands and wives have been in each other's company or society without rest or intermission for forty days, and the *New York Times* does not believe that this can be made to answer."

Whatever the case, laden with ninety pounds of biscuits, seventy pounds of canned meats and one hundred gallons of fresh water for making coffee, the *New Bedford* departed her namesake city to much fanfare and publicity, going first to Chatham on Cape Cod, where the height of the cabin was increased, some two hundred pounds of iron ballast was added and other minor details were attended to. The small craft was then towed out to sea and started her voyage to England on June 2, 1877. The boat was so small she didn't even qualify for registration papers, though Captain Crapo was given a certificate attesting to her size and homeport, as well as of his good intentions. During the subsequent voyage, many adventures were had along the way, including rough and stormy weather, pods of whales that came close enough to nearly upset the small boat and sightings and visits with many ships and steamers they encountered along the way. The nights were the hardest, as the sea was so black that nothing could be seen, and seasickness became a problem for Joanna. Still, the couple persevered, and though asked by the ships they encountered whether they desired to taken aboard and abort the voyage, they refused to do so. Finally, on July 21, after forty-nine days at sea, the *New Bedford* made landfall at Penzance, England.

The schooner-rigged whaleboat *New Bedford*, with Thomas and Joanna Crapo aboard while bound for England in 1877. *From Crapo's* Strange but True, *1893*.

The seafaring couple subsequently received a huge welcome in England and were well celebrated for their accomplishment. They and their boat were put on exhibit at several locales. Joanna Crapo in particular "was the lion of the hour. A woman to cross the tempestuous Atlantic Ocean in a small boat like ours was what turned the people's heads."

Upon their return to the United States by steamship in January 1878, the Crapos and their boat were exhibited on Broadway in New York for two weeks, after which they joined a famed circus and traveled to almost every New England state and as far west as Missouri. Captain Crapo, probably with the idea of making money quickly after suffering a financial loss when his own merchant ship was wrecked, conceived the idea of voyaging from New England to Cuba in a small nine-foot boat named the *Volunteer*. This time, however, Crapo's luck would run out, as while sailing off the Rhode Island coast, his boat was upset in a storm and Crapo was drowned. His body washed ashore in May 1899. Though the *New Bedford* was but a small boat that is now largely forgotten, she was, for a time, one of the most famous boats on both sides of the Atlantic.

SPRAY

The true-life story of Captain Joshua Slocum and his voyage alone around the world in the *Spray* from 1895 to 1898 is, quite simply, one of the most amazing feats in the annals of American maritime history. Indeed, Slocum's account of the voyage in his 1899 published book, *Sailing Alone Around the World*, is a remarkable story, a bestseller in its day and remains a classic of maritime literature that anyone reading this book should also read. A native of Nova Scotia, Slocum (1844–1909) began his maritime career at the age of fourteen when he shipped out as a cabin boy on a fishing schooner and eventually rose to command his own ships. However, by the 1890s, it was difficult for Captain Slocum to find a ship to command in the fast-declining age of sail. He was on the verge of going to work in a Boston shipyard when a friend, a retired whaling captain in Fairhaven, told him, "Come to Fairhaven and I'll give you a ship. But…she wants some repairs." With the idea of circumnavigating the globe in the right vessel, and even a publishing deal in place, Slocum was intrigued and went to Fairhaven. The vessel he was shown, the *Spray*, was a thirty-seven-foot-long fishing sloop, lying abandoned in a field some distance from the ocean. To say that the vessel needed repairs was an understatement to say the least, but Slocum right away knew that this was the vessel he had been looking for.

Little concrete is known about the *Spray* except that she had been registered in New Bedford and, according to historian Ken Slack, had previously been a sword-fishing boat owned at New Bedford and before that at Noank, Connecticut. She was a very common fishing sloop used on Long Island Sound. It seems likely that this "ancient" and abandoned ship, whose bones were still good, was at least twenty years old when Slocum found her. Whatever the case, the *Spray*, her original name retained out of tradition, was soon under repair by Slocum and his son. A nearby stand of white oak was used to replace her new stern post and replace her old-style centerboard with a keel, while Georgia pine was used for decking. The *Spray* had two cabins, one forward that measured six feet square and served as the galley and one aft measuring ten by twelve feet, more than enough room for the supplies Slocum would need. Once the *Spray* was back on the water and afloat, she was outfitted, as Slack notes, with "a smart stick of New Hampshire spruce" for her mast. The *Spray*, now brought back to life, had cost her new owner $553 and some thirteen months of his own labor.

Slocum subsequently departed Boston in April 1895 to begin his voyage. He first journeyed to his homeland of Nova Scotia for initial sea trials and from there began his ultimate adventure. His account of the voyage is a joy to read and backs up the statement by historian Frederick Matthews that "Captain Slocum was a first-class seaman and navigator, fearless and courageous." From an encounter with pirates off the coast of Morocco, a terrific storm and hostile Natives while passing through the Straits of Magellan, a period of seventy-two straight days without making landfall from Juan Fernandez Island to Samoa, rounding the Cape of Good Hope in stormy seas, acquiring a troublesome goat at St. Helena that nearly ruined his navigation in West Indies waters and, finally, passing Fire Island, New York, during a tornado before finally arriving at Newport, Rhode Island, in June 1898, Slocum seemingly saw it all during his thirty-eight-month voyage. While Slocum, the man, made it all happen, the soundly built *Spray*, a most common vessel, made it all possible. Slocum was the first to circumnavigate the globe alone, and though his achievement has been matched by others since then, those feats, though daring, had the advantage of modern-day vessels with the latest in navigational aids.

Sadly, as has happened with many other adventurers, the story of Slocum and the *Spray* does not have a happy ending. Just over ten years after his momentous voyage ended, in November 1909, Slocum's luck ran out when

The sloop *Spray*, which carried Captain Joshua Slocum around the world in 1895–98. *From Crowninshield's* Fore-and-Afters, *1940.*

he sailed from Massachusetts for the West Indies, with the hope of planning a new adventure on the Amazon River in South America. Slocum and the *Spray* never made port and disappeared without a trace; he was subsequently declared legally dead in 1924. However, through his amazing account, documented in a book that has seldom been out of print for over 120 years, the memory of Slocum and the *Spray* lives on.

IN THE SECOND PART of this chapter, we pay homage to some of the specially designed racing yachts that were built to defend the America's Cup, the most famed class of sport sailing ships in the world. These yachts flew the burgee of the New York Yacht Club, but they were designed and built in New England by two famed designers, Bostonian Edward Burgess (1848–1891) and marine architect Nathaniel Greene Herreshoff (1848–1938) of Bristol, Rhode Island. While it is true that the vast majority of Americans, then and now, have little in common with the so-called bluebloods—the ultra-wealthy individuals who owned and sailed these yachts, including the Morgans, the Vanderbilts and the Forbeses—it is also true that anyone with an affinity for sailing ships can appreciate these beautiful and innovatively designed vessels. Many, perhaps, can also appreciate a winner. The yachts designed by these men helped contribute greatly to the longest winning streak in sports history. The America's Cup was successfully held by the United States from 1851 to 1983, 132 years in all. The 1851 victory was defended twenty-four times before the Cup was finally lost to Australia in 1983. That's a dynasty greater than anything the New York Yankees or Boston Celtics have accomplished.

Edward Burgess got his start in 1885 when he designed the *Puritan*, following it up in 1886 with the *Mayflower* and in 1887 with *Volunteer* (which was built in Delaware)—three winners in the space of three years. Burgess was an interesting fellow, a Boston blueblood himself, the son of a wealthy shipping merchant who had grown up around ships and graduated from Harvard with a degree in entomology. Despite his love of bugs, so to speak, Burgess was well acquainted with those in Boston's yachting community and soon developed an interest and passion in marine architecture and even went to Europe to study the subject. Though technically an amateur, Burgess turned into a master upon devoting himself full time to yacht building in 1883 after his family fortune was lost. He became a celebrated figure with his three America's Cup defenders. Sadly, his was a shooting star, his reign lasting but five years before he died after contracting typhoid fever in 1891.

As for Nathaniel Herreshoff, he is an important figure in the history of marine and naval architecture overall and easily the most influential of the America's Cup designers, his reign in the sport lasting over twenty-five years. He graduated from the Massachusetts Institute of Technology (MIT) in 1870 with a degree in mechanical engineering. In 1878, he returned to his hometown and, with his brother, established the Herreshoff Manufacturing Company. Not only was Herreshoff—nicknamed "Captain Nat" and the "Wizard of Bristol"—an accomplished builder, but he was also a fine sailor. In the 1890s, the Herreshoffs turned to the yacht-building business, and beginning with *Vigilant* in 1893, he would design and build five America's Cup defenders, which also included *Defender*, *Columbia*, *Reliance* and *Resolute*, while two others, the *Enterprise* and the *Rainbow*, were built by his company, meaning that every winner of the America's Cup from 1893 to 1934 was built at his shipyard in Bristol. The secret to Herreshoff's success is that he was a true innovator who brought new technology to yacht building and design and wasn't afraid to push things to the limit, a no-nonsense type of guy, a typical old-school Yankee in many ways, blunt and opinionated. Herreshoff was also known as a designer who took every advantage of the existing rules regarding yacht design and specifications for America's Cup participants and used them to whatever advantage he could. In this regard, he has been compared by *Boston Globe* correspondent Kevin Hartnett to one of New England's greatest sports legends of the twenty-first century, coach Bill Belichick of the New England Patriots. Hartnett stated that Herreshoff, like Belichick, was "seeing possibilities within the existing rules that others didn't."

Puritan

The first of Edward Burgess's America's Cup yachts was the *Puritan*, which was built by George Lawley & Son in South Boston. She was launched in May 1885, being ninety-four feet long overall, just over eighty-one feet on the waterline, displacing some 105 tons and with a sail area of nearly eight thousand square feet. The wooden yacht has been termed in some old histories as a "compromise" design, combining elements of both British cutter-type yachts and those of American sloops. She would soon, according to historian Winfield Thompson, prove herself to be "at that time undoubtedly the fastest American yacht ever built." The *Puritan* was built for a Boston consortium of owners who fervently wished to provide a candidate for the defense of the America's Cup. However, she would have to beat out the New York Yacht Club's own contenders. As is usual when it comes to a New York and Boston sports rivalry, the trash-talking began right away, historian W.P. Stephens recounting that the New York press issued "contemptuous utterances…about 'brick' sloops and 'bean' boats that might better stay east of Cape Cod." In the subsequent three-race series, *Puritan* beat her rivals 2–1 and thus gained the honor of defending the Cup. The *Puritan*'s fight to retain the Cup was held against an English rival yacht, the *Genesta*, in September 1885, the winner taking the best in a three-race match. The first race was called off due to light winds, with *Puritan* ahead, but in the redo of that race, *Puritan* was at fault for colliding with the challenger while maneuvering at the start of the race. Though the race, by regulations, could have been awarded to the English boat, her owner did not want to win a race in that fashion and gracefully declined. After a few days for both yachts to make needed repairs, the race started again, and *Puritan* pulled steadily away for the win. In the second race, a close affair ensued, but *Puritan* beat her rival by less than two minutes, thereby keeping the America's Cup in American hands.

View of the 1885 America's Cup defender *Puritan*, designed by Edward Burgess of Boston. *Courtesy of the Library of Congress.*

COLUMBIA

Nathaniel Herreshoff's third foray into the America's Cup world began with the defense of the America's Cup in 1899. The contest pitted Scotsman Sir Thomas Lipton's *Shamrock* against Nat Herreshoff's *Columbia*. The yacht was built in the winter of 1898–99, made of bronze and steel and launched in June 1899. *Columbia* was said to be the most beautiful yacht ever built, measuring 140 tons and 132 feet long, 89 feet on the waterline, carrying 12,800 square yards of canvas. She had steel masts, which were lighter than the traditional pine masts and gave her increased speed. In the races that followed, *Columbia* easily won the first race and the second as well, as *Shamrock* had to withdraw after her topmast went by the way. In the anticlimactic third race, *Columbia* won easily yet again, and the Cup remained in America. However, in 1901, the two entrants would meet again, *Columbia* matched against Lipton's *Shamrock II*. The subsequent America's Cup match in September 1901 was an interesting one. The challenger lost in her first two

The two-time America's Cup defender *Columbia* (*left*), built by Nathaniel Herreshoff, racing against *Shamrock* in 1899. *Courtesy of the Library of Congress.*

races by a decent margin, and the last race was also a loss, but by less than a minute. This victory by *Columbia* marked the first time that the same yacht would win the America's Cup twice in a row, a feat that was not matched until 1970. Afterward, the former speedster was eventually broken up for her metal in 1915 at City Island, New York. Interestingly, the yacht *Columbia*, along with the Herreshoff yachts *Defender* and *Reliance*, was owned by famed yachtsman C. Oliver Iselin, and it was his wife, Hope Goddard Iselin, who also made Cup history. During the 1899 Cup defense by *Columbia*, Hope Iselin was aboard as part of the so-called afterguard crew with her husband. While she did not handle the sails, Iselin did serve in timing the yacht's run and is thought to be the first woman ever to sail in the America's Cup races.

Chapter 12

SURFACE WARSHIPS OF WORLD WAR II AND BEYOND

*I*n the aftermath of the attack on Pearl Harbor on December 7, 1941, the United States ramped up the production of all types of the military weapons that would be required to achieve victory during World War II. While these efforts had begun in earnest even before America's entrance into the war, beginning in 1939, it was when the clouds of war broke with such terrible force on that "date which will live in infamy," in President Franklin D. Roosevelt's immortal words, that the building of America's "arsenal of democracy" truly began, with results the like of which had never been witnessed before. Millions of weapons of all types were produced over the next four years, and when it came to naval vessels, New England helped to lead the way. Indeed, shipyards big and small from every New England state soon turned to the production of ships of all types to serve all branches of the service, including the U.S. Merchant Marine, Navy, Coast Guard and even Army, building over 1,550 ships during the war years.

These ships are classified into two types: capital warships, which played an offensive role in winning the war, as well as the smaller craft, of which many were also armed, that played a supporting role. These New England–built warships served and sacrificed in all theaters of the war. For example, the yard minesweeper *YMS-304*, built by Rice Brothers at East Boothbay, Maine, was mined and sunk off the Normandy coast in July 1944; the subchaser *PC-558*, built by Luders Marine in Stamford, Connecticut, was torpedoed and sunk off Salerno in May 1944 after having destroyed a German mini-submarine; and *LCI (L)-684*, built by the George Lawley Shipyard in Neponset, Massachusetts, was badly damaged by a kamikaze attack at Leyte Gulf in the Philippines in November 1944. However, it was the larger warships that really took the fight to the Axis powers, and after the war was over, many continued their service for years and conflicts to come.

The Fore River Shipyard in Quincy, Massachusetts, established in 1901 and by 1913 owned by Bethlehem Steel, was known for the big vessels it constructed during World War II. During this time, the shipyard had sixteen ways and employed about thirty-two thousand ship workers by 1943. It was so important to the build-up of the navy that early in the war, German U-boats lurked off its entrance, hoping to torpedo a newly built ship. However, in the years after the war, as the composition of our navy changed, the yard built fewer and fewer ships and finally closed in 1987. It is at the Bath Iron Works shipyard in Maine's "City of Ships" that the tradition of building capital surface ships has continued in New England. Bath Iron Works, established in 1884, is famed for the many destroyers it sent down the ways during World War II, when some fifteen thousand workers were employed. To this day, it is known for the destroyers and frigates it builds for the U.S. Navy, these ships the backbone of our modern naval forces.

USS Lexington (CV-2)

USS *Lexington* (CV-2) was just the second carrier ever built by the navy, originally laid down as a battlecruiser in early 1921 at the Fore River Shipyard. However, when it was just a quarter completed, *Lexington*'s construction was halted as a result of the Washington Naval Conference, where disarmament talks were held among nine nations, including the United States and Japan, and tonnage limits of warships for each country were established. The ship was subsequently redesignated as an aircraft carrier in July 1922, and construction continued.

When she was launched in 1925 and finally commissioned in 1927 as the lead ship in her class, she measured in at thirty thousand tons, 888 feet long, capable of carrying seventy-eight operational aircraft and manned by a crew of 2,800, including aircraft personnel. The *Lexington* was one of the largest aircraft carriers in the world at that time. During her operations prior to the war, the "Lady Lex" participated in many drills and fleet exercises in both the Atlantic and Pacific, including one in 1933 that simulated a carrier attack on Hawaii. One of her early commanders was future chief of naval operations Captain Ernest J. King.

On December 5, 1941, the *Lexington* departed Pearl Harbor under Captain Frederick Sherman, bound for Midway Island with a delivery of eighteen dive-bombers, thus missing the attack on Hawaii just two days later. The Japanese failure to catch any of the American carriers at Pearl was a circumstance that would soon prove costly and ultimately decide the outcome of the war. While *Lexington*'s role in World War II would be but fleeting, it was nonetheless historic. The *Lexington* in February 1942 was ordered to the area of the Coral Sea to help blunt the Japanese advance toward Australia. The *Lexington* saw her first real action of the war in her task force's raid on the Japanese stronghold of Rabaul, and despite heavy attacks by Japanese bombers, the *Lexington* and her crew fought them off. Later on, in concert with the carrier *Yorktown*, attacks by *Lexington*'s aircraft destroyed several transports, but subsequent severe weather curtailed operations, and *Lexington* was ordered back to Pearl Harbor. After a refit there, *Lexington* and her task force headed for sea again in April, subsequently directed to the Solomon Islands to help blunt the Japanese advance in that area with *Yorktown* and her task force.

On May 4, 1942, *Lexington* and *Yorktown* were ordered farther west into the Coral Sea. Opposed by three Japanese carriers, the action in what would be known as the Battle of the Coral Sea began on May 6, when the enemy carrier planes spotted and sank the destroyer USS *Sims* and badly damaged the large oiler USS *Neosho*. By later that day, both sides knew where the other's ships were, and the first carrier battle in history commenced. Aircraft from *Lexington* and *Yorktown* made attacks on the Japanese light carrier *Shoho*, with *Lexington*'s aircraft drawing first blood, hitting the carrier five times, before *Yorktown*'s aircraft finished her off. Struck by thirteen bombs and seven torpedoes, the flaming wreck of the *Shoho* soon went down, her demise noted by one of *Lexington*'s air group commanders, Lieutenant Commander Robert Dixon, who radioed back to *Lexington* the famous message "scratch one flattop." However, the battle was not yet decided, and the following day, both sides launched their carrier aircraft to seek out and destroy their opponents. While aircraft from *Yorktown* and *Lexington* found the carrier *Shokaku*, the damage their aircraft inflicted was but slight. Several hours later, Japanese bombers found their prey and commenced their attacks on *Lexington* just after 11:00 a.m., and though many of the attacking aircraft were shot down, several snuck through *Lexington*'s air cover and hit the carrier twice with their torpedoes. In a subsequent attack, the ship was again hit twice, this time by

The U.S. Navy aircraft carrier USS *Lexington* (CV-2), lost at the Battle of the Coral Sea in 1942. *Courtesy Naval History and Heritage Command archives.*

bombs, one of which detonated an ammunition locker, killing an entire gun crew and starting several fires. Despite the damage, the *Lexington* recovered her patrol aircraft and was preparing to launch another group just before 1:00 p.m. when a massive explosion sparked by gasoline vapors rocked the ship, followed by another an hour later. With her boilers shut down and the ship adrift, these further explosions and resulting fires doomed *Lexington*. Captain Sherman gave the order to abandon ship just after 5:00 p.m. This was done in an orderly fashion; many men were reluctant to leave until all their shipmates were accounted for. In all, 2,735 men were safely gotten off, but the burning *Lexington* refused to sink. Finally, just before 8:00 p.m., the destroyer USS *Phelps* fired five torpedoes into the *Lexington*, which finally caused the gallant carrier to sink.

To this day, many *Lexington* veterans are adamant in pointing out that the Japanese did not sink the Lady Lex. In all, the carrier lost 216 killed in the battle. Though this historic battle was technically a draw, the Battle of the Coral Sea was a tactical victory, the first time the Japanese advance in the Pacific would be stopped. It was also a lead-in to the subsequent

Battle of Midway just over a month later, a carrier battle that decided the outcome of the war in the Pacific. Interestingly, nearly seventy-six years later, in March 2018, the wreck of the *Lexington* was found, along with that of eleven aircraft, resting upright on the seafloor some ten thousand feet below the surface in an expedition conducted by philanthropist Paul Allen, her nameplate still clearly visible.

USS *Lexington* (CV-16)

One cannot talk about the first *Lexington* without discussing her successor, for the two ships are inexorably linked. This namesake carrier was laid down at the Fore River Shipyard in July 1941 and was launched in September 1942. Originally intended to be named the USS *Cabot*, her name was changed during construction after news of the loss of the original *Lexington* became known. Nicknamed the "Blue Ghost," this new *Lexington* was an *Essex*-class carrier, the most famed of any class of carriers to serve the U.S. Navy. She measured 27,100 tons and was 872 feet long, able to steam at a speed of thirty-three knots and built to carry 110 aircraft and manned by a crew of 2,600 men. Commissioned on February 17, 1943, the *Lexington*, after conducting shakedown and training exercises, transited the Panama Canal and arrived at Pearl Harbor in August 1943. She and her crew first saw action in September and October, raiding Tarawa and Wake islands, while in November her aircraft provided cover during the operation to liberate the Gilbert islands. At Kwajalein in December 1943, her aircraft destroyed numerous planes and damaged or sank three ships, though she herself was hit by a torpedo and had to return to Pearl Harbor for emergency repairs before heading stateside to Bremerton, Washington.

In March 1944, *Lexington* was back in action, now the flagship of Admiral Marc Mitscher and Task Force 58. In April, *Lexington* and her group conducted strikes in support of army landings at Hollandia and at the heavily defended Japanese base at Truk. Though heavily attacked, *Lexington* survived with nary a scratch, though Tokyo Rose would "report" on Japan's propagandist radio broadcasts for the second time now that *Lexington* had been sunk. In June, extensive operations were conducted at Saipan and in the Marianas. The carrier was reported by the enemy as being sunk again, though in fact the "Blue Ghost" continued her devastating strikes, conducting operations over Guam, the Palaus, the Caroline Islands, Mindanao, Okinawa and Formosa

(Taiwan) throughout the fall of 1944. In October 1944, *Lexington* and her air groups played a major role in the Battle of Leyte Gulf, a major victory in which her aircraft damaged three Japanese cruisers; sank one; helped sink the super-battleship *Musashi* and carriers *Chitose* and *Zuiho*; and on her own sank the carrier *Zuikaku*. This last sinking was a matter of pride perhaps, as well as revenge, for *Zuikaku* had been in action at the Battle of the Coral Sea, and her aircraft contributed to the sinking of the Lady Lex. However, not everything at the Battle for Leyte went the American way. Japanese kamikazes took their toll, including a hit on the *Lexington* that, though starting a number of fires aboard ship, did not curtail her action. Reported as being sunk yet again, *Lexington* steamed to Ulithi to repair her battle damage but was in action again by January 1945, performing airstrikes on Formosa, Okinawa, Saipan and Hong Kong and sinking some twenty vessels in convoys in Camranh Bay in Vietnam. In February, her airstrikes hit Tokyo and the Nansei Shoto in Japanese home waters, as well as airstrikes to soften opposition at Iwo Jima.

Following a brief refit stateside, *Lexington* was back in action again in July 1945 pounding the Japanese homeland naval and air bases, helping to cause the final destruction of the Japanese Imperial Navy, as well as industrial sites.

World War II view of aircraft recovery operations on the carrier USS *Lexington* (CV-16). *Courtesy Naval History and Heritage Command archives.*

Once the war ended in August, aircraft from *Lexington* still patrolled the skies over Japan, as well as dropping supplies to POW camps.

She finally headed stateside in December 1945, carrying a number of homeward-bound troops. Her wartime service ended, the *Lexington* and her crew had earned eleven battle stars and the Presidential Unit Citation for their extraordinary work. Subsequently homeported on the West Coast, in 1947 the veteran carrier was decommissioned, as so many warships were, and docked at Bremerton. She was eventually converted to an attack carrier and recommissioned in 1955 and served in the Far East until late 1962. She was sent to Pensacola, Florida, as a training carrier, but not before she was done patrolling the waters off Cuba during the Cuban Missile Crisis. From 1963 to 1991, she served as a training ship and was finally decommissioned in late 1991, the last of the famed *Essex*-class carriers to go out of service and the one that had served the longest. Upon her decommissioning, the carrier was given to the city of Corpus Christi, Texas, subsequently donated as a museum ship, in which capacity she still operates today. Deemed a National Historic Landmark in 2003, the old "Blue Ghost" is now the centerpiece of the USS *Lexington* on the Bay Museum and is well preserved and cared for, with many areas of the ship open to the public. Still riding the waves of Corpus Christi Bay, the *Lexington* is the oldest carrier still afloat in the world and an imposing sight to see.

USS MASSACHUSETTS (BB-59)

The day of the battleship was nearly at an end when the soon-to-be-nicknamed "Big Mamie" was launched in September 1941 at the Fore River Shipyard in Quincy, Massachusetts. The 38,580-ton battleship has the distinction of being the largest warship ever built at the shipyard and the largest ever built in New England. Once the main offensive firepower of any navy, battleships were overtaken by the aircraft carrier as the U.S. Navy's main offensive weapon in World War II. Still, battleships would prove invaluable during the war in the amount of firepower they could provide. and *Massachusetts* was one of the best. Commissioned and ready for service in May 1942, she was manned by a complement of 2,500 men and carried as her main armament nine sixteen-inch guns and twenty-five-inch guns, being 608 feet long and capable of making twenty-seven knots and a range of some fifteen thousand miles.

Her first combat assignment was with the Western Naval Task Force in the fall of 1942, sailing in support of Operation Torch, the invasion of North Africa. Being the flagship of Task Group 34.1, she first fired her guns during the naval Battle of Casablanca, the group's mission to knock out the Vichy French defenses of the port. At 7:00 a.m. on November 8, 1942, the *Massachusetts* became the first American ship to fire sixteen-inch shells during the war, trading volleys with the French battleship *Jean Bart*. The *Massachusetts* in this battle not only knocked out the French battleship, hitting her five times, but also aided in knocking out coastal batteries, an ammunition dump, merchant shipping in the inner harbor and even a drydock.

Following this action, the *Massachusetts* returned stateside and underwent a refit for subsequent operations in the Pacific. In March 1943, the battleship arrived in the Pacific at New Caledonia and from there provided support for operations throughout the Pacific. In July 1945, she was part of a battleship task force that bombarded Japanese homeland heavy manufacturing sites. In the heat of battle right to the end of the war, Big Mamie is said to have

Aerial view of the battleship USS *Massachusetts* off Boston, circa 1942. *Courtesy Naval History and Heritage Command archives.*

fired the last sixteen-inch shells of the war, and after the Japanese surrender, having earned eleven battle stars, she and her crew returned home in September 1945.

Overhauled at Puget Sound, *Massachusetts* subsequently sailed for Norfolk, Virginia, and was decommissioned there in 1947, never to see active duty again, being stripped for her parts before being stricken from the navy register in 1962. However, while she was slated to go to the scrapyard, some of her former crewmen intervened and formed the Massachusetts Memorial Committee to raise enough funds to buy the ship from the navy. This was achieved in 1965, and the *Massachusetts* was subsequently towed to her berth at Battleship Cove in Fall River, Massachusetts. Today, she is the focal point of an impressive museum that also includes the submarine *Lionfish* and the destroyer *Joseph P. Kennedy Jr.* Interestingly, though a museum ship for nearly twenty years, the battleship gave service of a sorts once again in the early 1980s when the navy recommissioned four *Iowa*-class battleships and needed material help in their outfitting, turning to the *Massachusetts* and several other battleships-turned-museums for badly needed parts. In 1986, the *Massachusetts* became a National Historic Landmark and was placed in the National Register of Historic Places.

USS *Portland* (CA-33)

Built at the Fore River shipyard from 1930 to 1932, this ten-thousand-ton heavy cruiser was named in honor of the city of Portland, Maine, though her sailors, in typical fashion, would come to call her "Sweet P." Her armament consisted of nine eight-inch guns, three each in two forward turrets and three in one rear turret, as well as an additional eight five-inch guns. When the United States entered World War II with the attack on Pearl Harbor, *Portland* was part of the *Lexington* task force headed toward Midway Island but thereafter was employed into April 1942 doing patrol duty between the West Coast of the United States and Hawaii. In April 1942, she was assigned to Task Force 17, centered on the carrier *Yorktown*, and in May, she screened the carrier during the Battle of the Coral Sea. She would subsequently undergo minor repairs and escort the wounded *Yorktown* back to Pearl Harbor and then take part in the historic Battle of Midway on June 4, 1942. She was part of *Yorktown*'s screen during that battle, but after the carrier was damaged by Japanese aircraft and later sunk, *Portland* received over two thousand of her crew and subsequently transferred them to another vessel for safe return.

After a return to Pearl Harbor, the cruiser was back in action again in early August as part of the Guadalcanal invasion force and, during the Battle of the Eastern Solomons, provided screening for the carrier USS *Enterprise*. After the battle, *Portland* escorted the carrier back to Pearl and subsequently took part in a raid with the light cruiser USS *San Juan* on Tarawa in October. Following this action, *Portland* was back with *Enterprise* and steamed back toward the Solomons, taking part in the Battle of the Santa Cruz Islands. There, she suffered her first battle damage after one of her own guns exploded but also provided excellent cover for her carrier, shooting down several attackers. During this battle, the cruiser was hit by three torpedoes from a Japanese submarine, but they failed to detonate, so the damage was minimal.

In mid-November, as part of Task Force 67, *Portland* saw major action during the naval Battle of Guadalcanal. After escorting a convoy from New Caledonia, the ships arrived at Guadalcanal and were unloading supplies when they were attacked unsuccessfully by Japanese aircraft. That same evening, November 12, 1942, *Portland* was part of a force of five cruisers and eight destroyers deployed to stop an approaching Japanese force of two battleships, a cruiser and eleven destroyers. The lead enemy destroyer was sunk by the American fleet almost immediately, but *Portland*, in the thick of things, was hit by a torpedo from a Japanese destroyer and had her rudder jammed and one of her gun turrets damaged. Forced to steam in circles because she could not steer, *Portland* nonetheless kept her guns trained on the enemy battleship *Hiei* and set the ship afire. Unable to withdraw because of her damage, along with two other ships, *Portland* the next day sank an already damaged and abandoned Japanese destroyer before finally making temporary repairs so that she once again could get underway. For her part in this battle, *Portland* earned a Meritorious Unit Commendation, having suffered eighteen men killed and a like number wounded.

After making Tulagi, the *Portland* was subsequently towed to Australia for repairs and later sailed for the Mare Island Navy Yard via Pearl Harbor, arriving there for repairs in March 1943. Once repaired and gaining new crew and undergoing training, the *Portland* returned to action, taking part in most major engagements, and was off Okinawa when the war ended. Her sixteen hard-earned battle stars made the ship and crew one of the most decorated units in the navy during the war. The *Portland* subsequently was flagship of a task force that accepted the surrender of the Caroline Islands,

Bow view of the heavy cruiser USS *Portland*, built at the Fore River Shipyard, Quincy, Massachusetts. *Courtesy Naval History and Heritage Command archives.*

with ceremonies taking place aboard ship, after which the cruiser was put on Magic Carpet duty, first bringing six hundred troops back to the United States from the Pacific and thereafter making two more voyages ferrying troops home from Europe in November and December 1945.

Subsequently decommissioned in 1946, *Portland* never sailed again and was struck from the navy register in 1959. Many historians have wondered how this veteran ship, which took part in every major battle in the Pacific during the entire war, was never saved as a museum ship. The only part of the gallant cruiser saved for posterity was her tripod mast, which still stands today in Portland, Maine's Fort Allen Park.

USS NICHOLAS (DD-449)

Built at the Bath Iron Works in Maine and launched in 1942, this destroyer would remain in the navy for twenty-eight years, serving in three wars and earning thirty battle stars, making her the most decorated ship in American naval history. One of the *Fletcher* class of "tin cans," the *Nicholas* displaced 2,050 tons and was manned by a crew of about 330 men. Armed with torpedoes, as well as five five-inch guns and ten forty-millimeter Bofors guns, and capable of making thirty-five knots, this ship, like others of her type, was tasked with a wide variety of duties, including escort and guard duty for convoys, providing fire support and protection in screening duties for larger ships and the antisubmarine work for which destroyers are noted. Arriving in the Pacific in late September 1942, *Nicholas* first saw duty at Guadalcanal. In July 1943, the destroyer took part in the Battle of Kula Gulf and earned the Presidential Unit Citation, being in the thick of battle and rescuing the nearly 300 survivors of the sunken cruiser USS *Helena*. Later that month, she took part in the Battle of Kolombangara, her task unit battling four enemy destroyers and disrupting Japanese amphibious operations.

After a refit stateside, the *Nicholas* returned to action in February 1944 and took part in numerous actions during the coming months, including sinking a Japanese submarine in mid-November while screening the cruiser USS *St.*

Bow view of the Bath, Maine–built destroyer USS *Nicholas*, shown here in camouflage paint scheme. *Courtesy Naval History and Heritage Command archives.*

Sister ships, destroyers USS *Nicholas* and USS *O'Bannon*, on the ways at Bath Iron Works in Maine, January 1942. *Courtesy Naval History and Heritage Command archives.*

Louis. From February to the end of the war, *Nicholas* was employed in a wide range of activities, including screening and antisubmarine work, as well as bombardment and convoy escort duty. Seemingly everywhere the action was in the Pacific, *Nicholas* earned sixteen battle stars in World War II. Little did anyone know that her career was far from over.

In August 1945, the *Nicholas* was in Tokyo Bay with the USS *Missouri* when the Japanese formally surrendered, and afterward, she carried American POWs home, arriving at Seattle in late October 1945. The *Nicholas* was decommissioned in 1946 but was brought back into service in 1951 for the Korean War, where she performed antisubmarine and carrier screening duty, as well as patrolling the Taiwan Strait. She served in the Far East into May 1953, earning another five battle stars. After being modernized in 1960, *Nicholas* was sent to the South China Sea for the first time since World War II to conduct operations. In 1965, she was employed in patrolling the South Vietnamese coast to prevent the smuggling of supplies, troops and weapons by the Viet Cong. The *Nicholas* would see extensive subsequent service during the Vietnam War providing gunfire support and doing patrol duty in the Gulf of Tonkin at the so-called Yankee Station and in the Mekong Delta, adding another nine battle stars to her credit.

In late 1968, the *Nicholas* saw more unusual duty when she was assigned to the Eastern Pacific for work in the Apollo Space Program for NASA, helping in the recovery of space capsules for the Apollo 7 and Apollo 8 missions. Having been the oldest destroyer in the navy since 1962, the end for *Nicholas* came in January 1970, when she was decommissioned at Pearl Harbor, complete with a ceremony recognizing her years of service.

Chapter 13

UNDERSEA WARRIORS, 1940–1969

New England's close association with submarine development began with David Bushnell and the *Turtle* during the Revolutionary War and continued in modern times with the formation of the Electric Boat Company in 1899. Irish immigrant inventor John Holland, living in New York, designed the navy's first five submarines, which were built in New Jersey and California, but would join his company with several others to establish the Electric Boat Company in Connecticut. One of his prototypes, the *Holland I*, is located in the Paterson Museum in Paterson, New Jersey today. While Holland envisioned the true submarine as an underwater vessel, shaped like a fish and designed to operate as such, his rival designer at Electric Boat, the former navy constructor Lawrence Spear, had other ideas, and soon Holland was out of the company. From the formation of the navy's Submarine Force in 1900 to the present, New England has been the primary provider of our country's submarines. In fact, the majority of U.S. submarines built during the war were constructed in New England, and without them, the war in the Pacific could not have been won. The two major builders were the Portsmouth Naval Shipyard in New Hampshire and the Electric Boat Company in Groton, Connecticut. Portsmouth built seventy-nine submarines during the war, while Electric Boat was just behind it, building seventy-eight boats. Portsmouth took its expertise to the extreme on January 27, 1944, when the yard launched three submarines at once—USS *Ronquil* (SS-396), USS *Redfish* (SS-395) and USS *Razorback* (SS-394)—

and a fourth submarine, USS *Scabbardfish* (SS-397), later in the same day. No other shipyard before or since has achieved this feat. Today, *Razorback* is preserved as the focal display of the Arkansas Inland Maritime Museum in North Little Rock.

Among the other submarines preserved as ship-museums in the United States that feature Portsmouth- or Groton-built wartime boats are *Pampanito* (SS-383), *Requin* (SS-481), *Bowfin* (SS-287), *Drum* (SS-228), *Torsk* (SS-423) and *Batfish* (SS-310), all built at Portsmouth; and *Cavalla* (SS-244), *Croaker* (SS-246), *Becuna* (SS-319) and *Cod* (SS-224), all built by Electric Boat. Such memorials are important in preserving the history of this special arm of the U.S. Navy, which suffered fifty-two boats lost and just over 3,500 men killed during the war. No other type of ship in the navy even came close to sacrificing so much for victory.

After World War II, these two shipyards would continue their excellence in submarine construction, turning to nuclear-powered boats beginning in the 1950s. It was those boats built in the 1950s and 1960s that did great work during not just the subsequent wars in Korea and Vietnam but also during the Cold War era, when many clashes between American and

The submarines USS *Redfish*, USS *Ronquil* and USS *Razorback* on the ways at the Portsmouth Naval Shipyard. *Courtesy Naval History and Heritage Command archives.*

Russian submarines took place in deep waters, usually in secretive events and operations outside the general knowledge of the public—except when disaster occurred. While Portsmouth would build its last submarine in 1969, the shipyard is still an important submarine repair base that is known for its expertise. As for Electric Boat, owned by the giant defense firm General Dynamics since the 1950s, it is building the navy's most modern submarines, having built ten of the *Virginia*-class fast-attack boats since 1999. This number includes one of the newest additions to the submarine fleet, the USS *Vermont* (SSN-792), which was commissioned without the usual fanfare in April 2020 because of the COVID-19 pandemic.

USS *Drum* (SS-228)

This submarine was built at the Portsmouth Naval Shipyard and commissioned on November 1, 1941, just over a month before America entered World War II. Though the twelfth boat by hull number in the famed *Gato* class of submarines, she was the first to be completed and see combat in the war. The boats of this class were the first submarines to be mass-produced and were the backbone of the wartime force that destroyed the Japanese merchant fleet. *Drum* made thirteen war patrols in the Pacific from April 1942 to April 1945 and was one of the most successful submarines in the war, sinking fifteen ships with an aggregate of just over 80,500 tons, with only seven boats sinking a higher amount of tonnage. For her service, the submarine earned twelve battle stars. On her first war patrol commencing in April 1942, the boat sank a large, 11,000-ton seaplane carrier, as well as three other cargo ships. After her first sinking, *Drum* and her crew suffered from severe Japanese countermeasures, being held below and depth-charged for some sixteen hours. In October 1942, during patrol number three, Drum sank three large merchant ships, once again afterward enduring a severe depth-charging from angry Japanese escort ships. During her fourth patrol in December 1942, *Drum* hit a Japanese carrier with two torpedoes, but that ship got away, and the submarine was subsequently depth-charged for several hours.

It's hard for anyone who hasn't served aboard, or even been aboard, a submarine to know what a depth-charge attack might be like, but imagine yourself in a tin can under water, with someone dropping an explosive charge from above and tracking you by sonar. One loud noise inside the boat gives your position away, so all is set for silent running. Even depth-charges that don't find the exact mark cause damage by the concussive impact. Light bulbs shatter, insulation is knocked out from around the boat's interior and small leaks are even started as the hull and everyone within is rent by the force of successive blasts. In between depth-charges, the attacker from above can be heard as its propellers swish through the water, like an angry attack dog searching out its prey, its sonar pinging around you in eerie fashion. And then there's the anxious anticipation of the next blast. Will it find its mark this time? Or can the boat silently move away from its attacker? The longer the attack goes on, another fear comes to the fore as the air inside the boat grows stale, and though all but essential personnel are minimizing activity to preserve oxygen, the boat's officers may be forced to make a difficult decision: head up from the depths and fight it out on the surface before the air runs out (sooner if the boat is damaged and cannot remain below) or continue to play cat-and-mouse. The final, fatal depth-charge is usually the one we never know about—a direct hit splitting the thin pressure hull of the submarine open like a sardine can, subsequently killing all within by explosion or drowning. For those boats that fail to return to port, the simple notation "missing with all hands" belies the fact that the end of a submarine is a violent affair. Lucky for *Drum*, the boat and her crew survived all such attacks like this that were part of a submariner's life during wartime.

One man aboard who was known for his morale-boosting efforts during these attacks was Officer's Cook First Class George Washington Lytle. This African American crewman made *Drum*'s first ten war patrols and earned the Bronze Star for his exemplary service, one of the few Blacks so honored in the navy during the war, for "cool courage and devotion to duty in the face of vigorous and persistent depth-charge attacks," which "enhanced the aggressive fighting spirit of the entire crew." During *Drum*'s eighth war patrol in November 1943, in an attack that damaged the boat so much that her entire conning tower had to be replaced, Lytle, stationed in the forward compartment, kept up the spirits of his fellow crew by recording each depth-charge dropped by making a mark on pinup girl Betty Grable's rear end on the wardroom calendar, an event remembered by *Drum* veterans nearly fifty years later. It should be no surprise, then, that while the navy and the Submarine Force were slow to recognize the contributions of African Americans during the war, when they did, former *Drum* crew member George Lytle would be the first Black man whose image and story were put on display in the Submarine Force Library and Museum in Groton, Connecticut, just after his death in 1987.

The *Gato*-class submarine USS *Drum*, built in 1941, here shown on the Potomac River before her retirement. *Courtesy Naval History and Heritage Command archives.*

Drum's eleventh war patrol in October 1944 served as a capstone to her outstanding career, the boat sinking three large enemy cargo and transport vessels during the Philippines campaign. She would end the war by providing lifeguard duty for air-strike operations off Okinawa and the Nansei Shoto. After the war, *Drum* would continue in reserve service until being retired in 1967 and struck from the Navy List in 1969. In that same year, the old veteran submarine was donated to the USS *Alabama* Battleship Museum and was towed to Mobile and opened up as a museum ship in July 1969. *Drum* for many years rode the waves in Mobile Bay, but after being damaged by a hurricane in 1998, she was moved to a shore berth. Since 2015, *Drum* has been almost fully restored and has been visited by thousands of people every year.

USS Albacore (AGSS-569)

Now a museum ship, this revolutionary submarine was a game-changer in the field of naval architecture and submarine hull design. Laid down at the Portsmouth Naval Shipyard in March 1952 and commissioned in December 1953, the 1,607-ton, 205-foot-long *Albacore* was designed with a new age in mind, one where submarines would be an increasingly important part of America's naval force and with the nuclear-powered submarine USS *Nautilus* already on the ways down at Electric Boat, a vessel that would soon operate primarily under water. Though powered by a pair of non-nuclear power plants that turned a single-screw propeller, the unique hull of *Albacore* was an experimental one that proved a great success. The auxiliary submarine was found to be capable of traveling thirty-three knots while submerged and twenty-five knots on the surface. In contrast, a wartime boat like *Drum* could do but nine knots submerged.

After several years of design testing at both the David Taylor Model Basin in Carderock, Maryland, and the wind-tunnel at Langley Air Force Base in Virginia, a teardrop-shaped hull form, often called the "Albacore hull," was decided on by the submarine's designers. Submarine pioneer John Holland would have been pleased indeed with the resulting streamlined and fish-like design, and in subsequent testing, *Albacore* would soon prove her hull form to be the standard for future boats. Once in commission, this submarine, which was unarmed and thus never fired a shot, was constantly employed in test evaluations, often in conjunction with antisubmarine units, even including one demonstration cruise with CNO Admiral Arleigh Burke aboard. The *Albacore* was a big deal, and it was an exciting time for submarine development. The boat often returned to Portsmouth for modifications. In 1956, the submarine was even filmed for a national television program, with an underwater camera mounted on her forecastle providing the first ever live footage of a submarine dive. Modifications to her stern, bow planes and even a newly designed fourteen-foot propeller prompted changes that were incorporated in new submarines that were being added to the fleet. In the 1960s, the *Albacore* would test new engines and a new sonar system, as well as many other technical aspects, and she would remain an active test platform for submarine design research into 1971.

The experimental submarine USS *Albacore*, built at Portsmouth in 1953, is now a museum ship. *Courtesy Naval History and Heritage Command archives.*

In 1972, the aging *Albacore* was retired and decommissioned at the Philadelphia Naval Yard and was finally struck from the naval register in 1980, having, as one naval research official stated, given "its body to science." Luckily, the submarine-minded town of Portsmouth, New Hampshire, would come together to save this unique vessel from the scrapyard. The Portsmouth Submarine Memorial Association was formed to bring the ship home. This it did in 1984 to much fanfare, a complicated and exciting project that I well remember. The submarine, named a National Historic Landmark in 1989, is berthed in a special dry basin so that her revolutionary hull form can be seen by all. Located in a highly visible spot off Market Street, the USS *Albacore*, the feature of Albacore Park, is a major attraction and visited by thousands every year.

USS *Nautilus* (SSN-571)

Famed as the world's first nuclear-powered ship of any kind, this submarine represented a major change in the U.S. Navy's Submarine Force and heralded the coming age of nuclear-powered warships. The *Nautilus* was named not only after a famed World War II submarine of the same name but also Jules Verne's fictional submarine *Nautilus* in his acclaimed 1870 science fiction novel *20,000 Leagues Under the Sea*. The submarine was the brainchild of Captain Hyman Rickover, known as the "Father of the Nuclear Navy," a visionary whose exacting standards for those serving in nuclear-powered boats were both fearsome and legendary. *Nautilus* was authorized by Congress in 1951, with her keel laid down by Electric Boat the following year. On January 21, 1954, the *Nautilus* was launched and was commissioned later that year in September. The Soviets would not commission their first nuclear submarine until 1961. However, there was work to be done. The *Nautilus* was first underway by her own power on January 17, 1955, when she departed Groton, Connecticut, with Commander Eugene Wilkinson radioing the famed message "Underway on nuclear power." The boat was subsequently completed in April 1955 and the following month departed Groton on a shakedown cruise, traveling some 1,400 miles to Puerto Rico entirely under water in under ninety hours. This was the longest submerged cruise ever by a submarine up to that time, as well as the fastest. The 3,500-ton submarine is 320 feet long, powered by a single nuclear reactor that drove twin propellers, manned by a crew of 105 men and armed with six torpedo tubes.

For the first two years of her career, *Nautilus* was employed in speed, endurance and antisubmarine testing in both the Atlantic and the Pacific, her high speed and capabilities rendering the submarine doctrines used in World War II obsolete. In April 1958, the boat, now captained by Commander William Anderson, departed New London, Connecticut, for the Pacific in advance of Operation Sunshine, a submarine transit of the North Pole under the ice. This operation was conceived as a result of the Soviet launch of its Sputnik I satellite in October 1957, an event that deeply embarrassed and worried the United States in general and its military leaders in particular. The epic voyage to transit the North Pole began on June 9, 1958, with the *Nautilus*'s departure from Seattle, but not before two interesting incidents occurred, as later recounted by Commander Anderson in his book about the voyage. The first of these regarded persistent leaks in the boat's condenser system during the run to Seattle. The captain gave thought to the problem and came up with an unusual solution. He directed his nuclear engineer, Commander Paul Early, to send out men to every gas station in the Seattle area to buy a common automobile remedy called Stop-Leak—without, of course, mentioning that it was for *Nautilus*. This his crew did, buying some 140 quarts of the stuff, spending about $250 to solve a problem on the most advanced ship in the world. As it turns out, the solution worked. Commander Anderson was also anxious before his voyage to get an aerial view of the ice conditions in the Bering Strait. To that end, he used a forged identity card that had previously been supplied to book a flight on a small commercial airliner up to Alaska. This did the job, though on the way back, the plane unexpectedly ran low on fuel and was forced to land at a small village airstrip. The commander made it back to *Nautilus* one day before her departure for Alaska. Prior to her departure, Commander Anderson also had the hull number of *Nautilus* blacked out on her sail and bow. His orders were to make the voyage in secret and, if detected, to conceal the identity of the boat. The first attempt, however, was blocked by pack ice, so *Nautilus* turned back and put in at Pearl Harbor. In late July, *Nautilus* resumed the transit mission, with many worries in hand, including possible problems in navigation and having to surface from beneath the ice, perhaps using her torpedoes to blow a passageway. In the Bering Strait, especially, the room between the pack ice and the sea floor was very problematic, but *Nautilus* made it and reached the top of the world, ninety degrees north, on August 3, subsequently completing the transit of the North Pole two days later on August 5 and then reaching Jan Mayen Island in the Arctic Ocean on the next day—the first land sighted since Alaska had been left behind. With

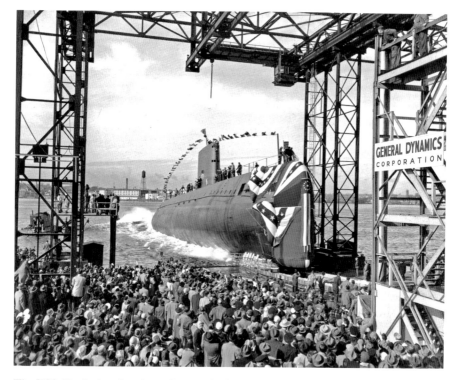

The USS *Nautilus* heading down the ways in Connecticut, the world's first nuclear-powered warship. *Courtesy Naval History and Heritage Command archives.*

this historic voyage, *Nautilus* had accomplished in reverse a passage that European maritime explorers had previously dreamed of for hundreds of years. For this extraordinary performance, the boat and crew were awarded the Presidential Unit Citation.

Following this voyage, *Nautilus* carried out her regular duties for the next nineteen years. However, by 1979, the submarine pioneer was outdated and ready to be retired. She was decommissioned and stricken from the Navy List in March 1980. However, the career of the *Nautilus* was far from over. Designated a National Historic Landmark in 1982, *Nautilus* was towed to Groton, Connecticut, in 1985 after having undergone a conversion process, and in 1986, she was opened to the public as a museum ship, a key feature of the Submarine Force Library and Museum. Today, several portions of the *Nautilus* are open to the public, and the boat is visited by thousands of people every year.

USS *Thresher* (SSN-593) AND USS *Scorpion* (SSN-589)

The decade of the 1960s was a very active one for the U.S. Navy's Submarine Force, one that saw increased design development as the role of the submarine quickly evolved. During the decade, there was much daring, adventure and constant danger as the Cold War took a serious turn under water, but also tragedy. The two submarines *Thresher* and *Scorpion* are bookends of a sort to the decade, serving perhaps as a cautionary tale and reminding the nation that, as advanced as our submarine program was, and no matter how great our military capabilities may be, sometimes our advances came at a high cost.

USS *Thresher* was laid down at the Portsmouth Naval Shipyard in May 1958, launched in July 1960 and commissioned in August 1961. She was the lead boat of a new class of nuclear attack submarines that were created with the main task of hunting down and destroying Soviet submarines. Displacing 3,200 tons and 279 feet long, with a crew of 112 men and officers and capable of traveling at a speed of thirty-three knots, *Thresher* was the fastest and quietest submarine in the fleet, armed with the navy's newest antisubmarine missiles. It was anticipated that some twenty-five boats of this class would be built, so satisfactory was her design perceived to be on initial delivery. Upon her finishing, the boat conducted sea trials in the Atlantic and the Caribbean, as well as nuclear submarine exercises in 1961–62. In July 1962, *Thresher* was in drydock at Portsmouth for a post-shakedown examination and overhaul, a process that took some nine months because she was the first boat in a new class of submarines. The ship was subsequently certified to return to sea on April 8, 1963, and the following day headed out to sea under the command of Lieutenant Commander John Harvey for post-overhaul dive trials. These took place some 220 miles east of Cape Cod. On board with *Thresher*'s crew were a number of civilian experts and technicians. In the early hours of April 10, *Thresher* began a deep dive to test her systems, reporting every 100 feet to a submarine rescue tender that accompanied her. Near her test depth, minor difficulties were encountered and radioed by the submarine back to her escort, but the transmission was garbled. When the submarine apparently reached 900 feet, another garbled message was received, but thereafter, *Thresher* was silent. It was quickly realized that the boat had sunk, and soon over a dozen navy vessels arrived on the scene to conduct search-and-rescue operations, but nothing could be done. By the morning of April 11, 1962, *Thresher* was posted as missing with all 129 of her crew and shipyard personnel aboard.

This tragic event, the loss of the navy's newest and most powerful submarine, shocked the nation and stunned all of New England, especially the local New Hampshire and Maine area where she had been built. Deep-sea operations in June 1964 found the wreck of *Thresher*, and by the next month, most of it had been photographed. Subsequent investigations and reviews of her operational history and overhaul work have attributed the cause of her loss to a piping failure, with the welded joints on her salt-water piping system deemed defective, leading to a possible chain of events that included a loss of power and inability of the submarine to blow her ballast tanks. It is likely that following these circumstances, the *Thresher* plunged to the bottom of the ocean, imploding somewhere at a depth of 1,300 to 2,000 feet. Dr. Robert Ballard, the oceanographer famous for exploring the wreck of the *Titanic*, found the remnants of *Thresher* in the early 1980s, with only mangled wreckage remaining. The loss of the *Thresher*, which remains in commission to this day, was a real shock to the navy and resulted in many changes. The memory of the *Thresher* in the Portsmouth-Kittery area today remains strong. Her loss is memorialized annually, and many are still able to recall that fateful day so long ago when she went missing.

The USS *Scorpion* would have a different and somewhat longer career than the *Thresher*, but the end result would be the same—a destroyed submarine lying at the bottom of the Atlantic Ocean. *Scorpion* was laid down at the Electric Boat Yard in Groton, Connecticut, in 1958, launched in December 1959 and commissioned in July 1960. She was the third boat in the *Skipjack* class of nuclear submarines. *Scorpion* measured 2,900 tons and was 252 feet long, manned by a crew of anywhere from eighty-two to one hundred men. Upon her commissioning, *Scorpion* was homeported first out of Connecticut and later Norfolk. She completed a European deployment as well as fleet and NATO exercises, earning a Navy Unit Commendation. In subsequent years, the boat was employed in developing submarine warfare tactics and completed a number of patrols in the Atlantic and in European waters, including special operations off the coast of Russia. While many of her operations are still classified, much of her work certainly involved tracking Russian submarine activity during this heightened period of the Cold War.

In 1967, the *Scorpion* was due for a thorough overhaul, but because of cost-cutting measures, all but emergency repairs were deferred, including, incredibly enough, some repairs and changes planned as a result of the *Thresher* disaster. In any case, *Scorpion* returned to sea in the fall of 1967 under her new commanding officer, Commander Francis Slattery, then the youngest commander ever of a nuclear submarine. After training

Above: The ill-fated USS *Thresher*, built at Portsmouth 1959–60, lost during a test dive in 1963. *Courtesy Naval History and Heritage Command archives.*

Opposite: Rare photo of USS *Scorpion* prior to final departure, Rota, Spain, 1968. Captain Slattery is up top. *Courtesy Naval History and Heritage Command archives.*

exercises, the submarine sailed for the Mediterranean in February 1968 for operations in conjunction with the U.S. Sixth Fleet. By this time, the *Scorpion* had so many deficiencies that some of her crew nicknamed her the "USS Scrapiron," among them being the hatch for her trash-disposal unit that opened to the sea. No matter, the *Scorpion* performed her duty overseas into May 1968, though suffering a number of malfunctions, and her depth was said to be limited to five hundred feet. The submarine departed the Med for her home at Norfolk, stopping at the naval station in Rota, Spain, to drop off two crewmen for health and family-related issues. One final view of the submarine prior to her departure shows Captain Slattery on top of the sail with a bullhorn, directing crew operations. When *Scorpion* departed Spain, she was possibly providing cover for an American missile boat also leaving Rota at the same time, as Soviet submarines were known to be operating in the waters off the base. *Scorpion* was tasked with observing Soviet naval operations off the Azore Islands before returning homeward and performed this duty, observing, among other vessels, a Soviet *Echo II*–class submarine.

On May 21, *Scorpion* radioed that she was closing in on the Soviet submarine and other vessels, but thereafter, she was never heard from again. Subsequently declared overdue at Norfolk by May 27, the submarine was afterward presumed lost by June 5 and stricken from the Navy List on June 30, her ninety-nine-man crew declared dead. In fact, the navy knew the submarine was lost well before the public did, as the SOSUS underwater surveillance system detected the sound signature of the *Scorpion*'s underwater destruction. The navy subsequently sent a research ship to the area off the Azores where *Scorpion* was lost in October 1968 and found the wreck of the submarine in about ten thousand feet of water, the boat split in two and the hull folded inward, her sail ripped off the hull. A navy inquiry into her loss failed to establish a cause, and to this day, at least officially, no cause has been determined. Some believe a torpedo malfunction destroyed the boat, while some believe the failure of the trash-disposal unit allowed water to enter her hull, which sank the boat. Still others attribute the loss to a hydrogen explosion, but the most intriguing possibility is that *Scorpion* was destroyed by a Russian submarine as a retaliatory act for another submarine loss during Cold War operations. In fact, in 1968, four submarines were lost, three of them nuclear submarines, which included one French submarine, one Russian and *Scorpion*. The Russian submarine *K-129* was lost with all hands in the Pacific in March 1968, just two months prior, and while the U.S. Navy denied responsibility, many Soviets believed the United States was responsible. It has further been speculated that the Soviets responded when they had the chance by sinking *Scorpion*.

Was the submarine really sunk as a result of a confrontation with a Soviet submarine? To this day, the answer is unknown but certainly a possibility and, in my opinion, the most likely cause. It has been stated by some sources that after this event, both the Soviet and American governments called a truce of sorts and covered up the true nature of the chain of events. Despite the tragic losses of *Thresher* and *Scorpion*, it is important to note that no American submarines have been lost since that time. In this manner, perhaps, they and their long-lost crews are still doing their duty and, as all lost submarines are, still on Eternal Patrol.

BIBLIOGRAPHY

Anderson, Commander William R., and Clay Blair Jr. *Nautilus 90 North*. Cleveland, OH: World Publishing Co., 1959.

Baker, William Avery. *A Maritime History of Bath, Maine and the Kennebec River Region*. Vols. 1–2. Bath, ME: Marine Research Society of Bath, 1973.

Blair, Clay, Jr. *Silent Victory: The Submarine War Against Japan*. Philadelphia: J.B. Lippincott, 1975.

Bradlee, Francis B.C. *Some Account of Steam Navigation in New England*. Salem, MA: Essex Institute, 1920.

Briggs, L. Vernon. *History of Shipbuilding on the North River, Plymouth County, Massachusetts*. Boston: Coburn Brothers, 1889.

Chapelle, Howard I. *The History of the American Sailing Navy*. New York: Bonanza Books, 1949.

Colton, Tim. "Shipbuilding History—Construction Records of U.S. and Canadian Shipbuilders and Boat Builders." shipbuildinghistory.com.

Crapo, Thomas. *Strange but True: Life and Adventures of Captain Thomas Crapo and Wife*. New Bedford, MA: Thomas Crapo, 1893.

Crowninshield, B.B. *Fore-and-Afters*. Boston: Houghton Mifflin, 1940.

Cussler, Clive, and Craig Dirgo. *The Sea Hunters II*. New York: Berkley Books, 2004.

Cutler, Carl C. *Greyhounds of the Sea: The Story of the American Clipper Ship*. New York: Halcyon House, 1930.

Dow, George Francis. *Whale Ships and Whaling*. Salem, MA: Marine Research Society, 1925.

Fairburn, William Armstrong. *Merchant Sail*. Vols. 1–6. Lovell Center, ME: Fairburn Marine Educational Foundation, 1945–55.

Gibson, Gregory. *Demon of the Waters: The True Story of the Mutiny on the Whaleship* Globe. Boston: Little, Brown, and Co., 2001.

Hall, Henry. *Report on the Ship-Building Industry of the United States*. Washington, D.C.: GPO, 1884.

Hartnett, Kevin. "Nathaniel Greene Herreshoff, the Bill Belichick of Yacht Design." *Boston Globe*, September 15, 2015. www.bostonglobe. com/ideas/2015/09/15/nat-herreshoff-bill-belichick-yacht-design/ uqcLvMP5r3LTB7h97C73tI/story.html.

Hohman, Elmo Paul. *The American Whaleman*. New York: Longmans, Green and Company, 1928.

Howe, Octavius, and Frederick C. Matthews. *American Clipper Ships 1833–1858*. Vols. 1–2. New York: Dover Publications, 1986.

Knoblock, Glenn A. *The American Clipper Ship, 1845–1920*. Jefferson, NC: McFarland & Co., 2014.

———. *Black Submariners in the United States Navy, 1940–1975*. Jefferson, NC: McFarland & Co., 2005.

Lampson, Charles R. "Privateers of the Revolution." Massachusetts Society Sons of the American Revolution, June 23, 2011. www.massar. org/2011/06/23/privateers-of-the-revolution/.

Lubbock, Basil. *The Down Easters: American Deep-Water Sailing Ships*. Boston: Charles E. Lauriat Co., 1930.

Maclay, Edgar S. *A History of American Privateers*. New York: D. Appleton and Co., 1899.

Matthews, Frederick C. *American Merchant Ships 1850–1900*. Series I and II. New York: Dover Publications, 1987.

McKay, Richard C. *Some Famous Sailing Ships and Their Builder Donald McKay*. New York: G.P. Putnam, 1928.

Mjelde, Michael Jay. *Glory of the Seas*. Middletown, CT: Wesleyan University Press, 1970.

Morison, Samuel Eliot. *The Maritime History of Massachusetts, 1783–1860*. Boston: Houghton Mifflin, 1921.

Morris, Paul C. *American Sailing Coasters of the North Atlantic*. New York: Bonanza Books, 1979.

Morrison, John H. *History of American Steam Navigation*. New York: W.F. Sametz and Co., 1903.

Naval History Division. *United States Submarine Losses World War II*. Washington, D.C.: Office of the Chief of Naval Operations, 1963.

Osgood, Charles H., and H.M. Batchelder. *Historical Sketch of Salem 1626–1879*. Salem, MA: Essex Institute, 1879.

Paine, Ralph D. *The Ships and Sailors of Old Salem*. Chicago: A.C. McClurg, 1912.

Parker, W.J. Lewis. *The Great Coal Schooners of New England*. Mystic, CT: Marine Historical Association, December 1948.

Peabody, Robert. *The Log of the Grand Turks*. Boston: Houghton Mifflin, 1926.

Roscoe, Theodore. *United States Destroyer Operations in World War II*. Annapolis, MD: U.S. Naval Institute, 1966.

Rowe, William H. *The Maritime History of Maine*. New York: W.W. Norton & Co., 1948.

Saltonstall, William. *Ports of Piscataqua*. Boston: Harvard University Press, 1940.

Slack, Kenneth E. *In the Wake of the Spray*. New Brunswick, NJ: Rutgers University Press, 1966.

Slocum, Captain Joshua. *Sailing Alone Around the World*. New York: Century Co., 1900.

Smith, Eugene. *Passenger Ships of the World Past and Present*. Boston: George H. Dean, 1963.

Smith, Philip Chadwick Foster. *The Empress of China*. Philadelphia: Philadelphia Maritime Museum, 1984.

Sontag, Sherry, Christopher Drew and Annette Lawrence Drew. *Blind Man's Bluff: The Untold Story of American Submarine Espionage*. New York: Public Affairs Books, 1998.

Spears, John R. *Captain Nathaniel Brown Palmer: An Old-Time Sailor of the Sea*. New York: Macmillan Company, 1922.

Stanton, Samuel Ward. *American Steam Ships*. New York: Smith & Stanton, 1895.

Starbuck, Alexander. *History of the American Whale Fishery*. Secaucus, NJ: Castle Books, 1989 (facsimile of the 1877 edition).

State Street Trust Company. *Old Shipping Days in Boston*. Boston: State Street Trust, 1918.

Stephens. W.P. *American Yachting*. New York: Macmillan Company, 1904.

Thomas, Gordon W. *Fast & Able: Life Stories of Great Gloucester Fishing Vessels*. Gloucester, MA: William Brown, 1952.

Thompson, Winfield M., and Thomas W. Lawson. *The Lawson History of the America's Cup*. Southampton, UK: Ashford Press Publishing, 1986.

Toppan, Andrew, ed. "DANFS Online: The Dictionary of American Naval Fighting Ships." www.hazegray.org/danfs.

Winslow, Richard E., III. *Portsmouth-Built: Submarines of the Portsmouth Naval Shipyard*. Portsmouth, NH: Portsmouth Marine Society—Peter Randall, Publisher, 1985.

ABOUT THE AUTHOR

*H*istorian Glenn A. Knoblock is the author of *The American Clipper Ship* and eight books with Arcadia and The History Press, including *New Hampshire Covered Bridges*, *Brewing in New Hampshire* (with James Gunter) and *Historic Burial Grounds of the New Hampshire Seacoast*. He resides in Wolfeboro Falls, New Hampshire.